lonely planet

POCKET

VANCOUVER

TOP EXPERIENCES • LOCAL LIFE

D1262795

JOHN LEE

Contents

Plan Your Trip 4

Steam Clock (p67)
JAMES WHEELER / 500PX ©

Explore
Vancouver 31

COVID-19

We have re-checked every business in this book before publication to ensure that it is still open after the COVID-19 outbreak. However, the economic and social impacts of COVID-19 will continue to be felt long after the outbreak has been contained, and many businesses, services and events referenced in this guide may experience ongoing restrictions. Some may be temporarily closed, have changed their opening hours and services, or require bookings; some unfortunately could have closed permanently. We suggest you check with venues before visiting for the latest information.

Survival
Guide 147

Special Features

Vancouver's Top Experiences

Walk the Stanley Park seawall (p34)

KUMARAMV / SHUTTERSTOCK ©

See the forest of totem poles at the Museum of Anthropology (p132)

Brave the leg-wobbling Capilano Suspension Bridge (p56)

Dress up for a Vancouver Art Gallery social evening (p38)

Entertain the whole family at Science World (p100)

Snack your way around the Granville Island Public Market (p78)

DEYMOSHR / SHUTTERSTOCK ©

Get your true crime fix at the Vancouver Police Museum (p60)

JOHN MITCHELL / ALAMY STOCK PHOTO ©

Bask in the calm of Dr Sun Yat-Sen Classical Chinese Garden (p62)

Watch eagles and turtles in VanDusen Botanical Garden (p116)

Dining Out

Vancouver has an eye-popping array of generally good-value dining options: authentic Asian restaurants, finger-licking brunch spots, fresh-catch seafood joints and a locally sourced farm-to-table scene are all on the menu here. Follow your taste buds and dinner will become the talked-about highlight of your Vancouver visit.

CANNON PHOTOGRAPHY LLC / ALAMY STOCK PHOTO ©

Seafood

One reason Vancouver has great sushi is the larder of top-table regional seafood available right off the boat. Given the length of British Columbia's coastline, it's no surprise most restaurants find plenty of menu space for local salmon, halibut, spot prawns and freshly shucked oysters. If you're a seafood fan, you'll be in your element; even fish and chips are typically excellent. Start your aquatic odyssey at Granville Island, where the Public Market has seafood vendors and Fisherman's Wharf is just along the seawall.

Asian Smorgasbord

Vancouver (and the adjoining city of Richmond) is home to the best Asian dining outside Asia. From authentic sushi and ramen spots to lip-smacking hot pot and *banh mi* sandwich joints, you'll be spoilt for choice. Adventurous foodies should combine award-winning restaurants with smaller mom-and-pop places.

Veggie Hot Spots

Vancouver's vegan and vegetarian dine-out scene has entered a taste-tripping golden age. A full menu of delicious meat-free eateries has popped up and many are luring carnivores with their hearty comfort-food dishes like burgers and brunches. Keen to adopt a more plant-based diet? This is the city to kick things off in.

JOHN LEE / LONELY PLANET ©

Best Breakfast

Paul's Omelettery Neighborhood haunt specializing in breakfast. (p123)

Jam Cafe Tempting breakfast and brunch dishes. (p48)

Save On Meats Retro-look diner with a cool long counter. (pictured above left; p69)

Best Vegetarian

Acorn The city's best veggie restaurant. p104)

MeeT in Gastown Vegan comfort dishes in a chatty backstreet setting. (p70)

Naam Kitsilano vegetarian legend, open 24 hours. (p141)

Best Asian

Anh & Chi Contemporary Vietnamese restaurant loved by hungry locals. (p104)

Heritage Asian Eatery Well-priced top-notch rice bowls and more. (p124)

Bao Bei Supercool modern Chinese dining. (p70)

Best Happy Hour Dining Deals

Tacofino Taco Bar 3pm to 6pm daily (p68)

Jamjar Canteen 4pm to 6pm daily (p141)

La Taquería Pinche Taco Shop 3pm to 6pm daily (pictured above; p123)

Street-Food-A-Palooza

A late starter to the North American street-food movement, Vancouver now has one of the tastiest scenes in Canada. On most days, the downtown core has the highest concentration of trucks. You'll find everything from Korean sliders to salmon tacos, Thai green curry to barbecued brisket sandwiches. Check out what's on the street during your visit at www.streetfoodapp.com/vancouver.

Bar Open

Vancouverites spend a lot of time drinking. And while British Columbia (BC) has a tasty wine sector and is undergoing an artisanal distilling surge, it's the regional craft-beer scene that keeps many quaffers merry. For a night out with a side dish of locally made libations, join city drinkers in the bars of Gastown, Main St and beyond.

Craft Beer

Vancouver is one of Canada's craft beer capitals, with dozens of producers to discover. Plan an easy stroll around a cluster of microbrewery tasting rooms on and around Main St. Radiating from the northern end of Commercial Dr, you'll discover another easy-to-explore area sometimes called 'Yeast Vancouver.' For more information on local beery happenings, visit www.camravancouver.ca.

Wine & Liquor

It's not just beer that's raised the bar here. Grape-based quaffing kicked off the drinking revolution and while the cocktail scene took longer, it now combines quirky nightspots with sleek high-end options. Adding to your options, distinctive craft distilleries have also popped up. Vancouver's happy-hour rules mean that you can afford to be adventurous.

Alternative Night Out Ideas

Pick up a copy of the free *Georgia Straight* weekly, the city's best listings newspaper, for night-out ideas. Consider FUSE party nights at the Vancouver Art Gallery (p38); table tennis at Back and Forth Bar (p72); and the Regional Assembly of Text (p110)'s monthly letter-writing club.

LAWRENCE WORCESTER / LONELY PLANET LPI COLLECTION ©

Best Beer Bars

Alibi Room Vancouver's fave craft-beer tavern, with around 50 mostly BC drafts. (p72)

Railway Stage & Beer Cafe Upstairs bar with a good array of BC taps. (pictured; p50)

Best Happy Hours

Liberty Distillery 3pm to 6pm Monday to Thursday. (p90)

Uva Wine & Cocktail Bar 2pm to 5pm daily. (p50)

Keefer Bar 5pm to 7pm Sunday to Friday. (p73)

Sing Sing Beer Bar 3pm to 6pm daily. (p108)

Best for Cocktails

Shameful Tiki Room Windowless tiki-themed cave with strong concoctions. (p107)

Keefer Bar Chinatown's favourite lounge with great drinks and a cool-ass vibe. (p73)

Liberty Distillery Granville Island craft producer with a cool saloon-look bar. (p90)

Best Bar Patios

Six Acres Small patio in Gastown's coziest tavern. (p73)

Narrow Lounge Tiny 'secret garden' back area with intimate party vibe. (p107)

Best Bar Food

Alibi Room Hearty elevated comfort food and an excellent selection of beers. (p72)

Treasure Hunt

Vancouver's retail scene has developed dramatically. Hit Robson St's (pictured left) mainstream chains, then discover the hip, independent shops of Gastown, Main St and Commercial Dr. Granville Island is stuffed with artsy stores and studios. South Granville and Kitsilano's 4th Ave serve up a wide range of tempting boutiques.

I VIEWFINDER / SHUTTERSTOCK ©

Independent Fashion

Head off the beaten path to Main St or Commercial Dr for quirky vintage and artsy fashions. Or peruse the main drags of Gastown, South Granville and Kitsilano's 4th Ave for boutique gems. Watch for pop-up shops and check the pages of *Vancouver* magazine and the *Georgia Straight* for events such as Gastown's 'shop hops' – seasonal evenings of late openings with a partylike vibe. Before you arrive, see Vancouver fashion blogs www.alicia fashionista.com and www.tovogueorbust. com for the local lowdown.

Arts & Crafts

There are dozens of intriguing private galleries here, showcasing everything from contemporary Canadian art to authentic First Nations carvings and jewelry. There are also opportunities to buy art from local creatives at Granville Island's many artisan studios. In addition, there are dozens of arts and crafts fairs throughout the year. Check listings publications or www. gotcraft.com for upcoming events.

Souvenirs

Vancouver visitors have traditionally returned home with suitcases full of maple-sugar cookies. But it doesn't have to be this way. Swap that Gastown-clock fridge magnet for authentic First Nations jewelry; a book on Vancouver's eye-popping history (*Sensational Vancouver* by Eve Lazarus, for example) or a quirky Vancouver-designed T-shirt from the Main St fashion stores.

JOHN LEE/LONELY PLANET ©

Best Shops

Regional Assembly of Text Brilliantly creative stationery store with a little gallery nook. (pictured above; p110)

Pacific Arts Market Friendly gallery space showcasing dozens of regional creatives. (p128)

Red Cat Records Main St music store legend. (p109)

Best Bookshops

Paper Hound Perfectly curated, mostly used, downtown bookstore. (p52)

Massy Books Tome-lined Chinatown shop with secret bookcase nook. (p74)

Kidsbooks Giant, child-focused bookstore. (p145)

Pulpfiction Books Vancouver's favorite multi-branch secondhand-book store. (p113)

Best Record Shops

Red Cat Records Cool array of vinyl and CDs. (p109)

Neptoon Records Classic vinyl-focused store, perfect for browsing. (p111)

Zulu Records Giant selection in a *High Fidelity*–like setting. (p145)

Best Vintage Shopping

Mintage Mall Upstairs shared vendor space, located in Mount Pleasant. (p111)

Eastside Flea Vintage clothes and crafts at this regular event. (p74)

Best Arts & Crafts

Pacific Arts Market Upstairs gallery lined with the works of dozens of artists and artisans. (p128)

Bird on a Wire Creations Irresistible selection of artisan-made goodies. (p111)

Urban Source Create your own masterpiece via this beloved craft store. (p110)

Show Time

You'll never run out of options if you're looking for a good time here. Vancouver is packed with activities from high- to lowbrow, perfect for those craving a play one night, a hockey game the next, and a rocking poetry slam to follow. Ask the locals for tips and they'll likely point out grassroots happenings you never knew existed.

JSMIMAGES/ALAMY©

Live Music

Superstar acts typically hit the stages at sports stadiums and downtown theaters while smaller indie bands crowd tight spaces around town. Local record stores offer the lowdown on venues and acts to catch. Vancouver has wide musical tastes and, with some digging, you'll find jazz, folk, classical (Vancouver Symphony Orchestra pictured above right) and opera performances around the city.

Theater

Vancouver has a long history of treading the boards. The **Arts Club Theatre Company** (☎604-687-1644; www. artsclub.com; tickets from $29; ☺Sep-Jun) is the city's leading troupe, with three stages dotted around the city. Also consider January's **PuSh Festival** (www.pushfestival.ca; tickets from $10; ☺mid-Jan) and September's **Vancouver Fringe Festival** (www.vancou verfringe.com; Granville Island; tickets from $12; ☺Sep; 🚌50).

Film

There are plenty of places to catch blockbusters as well as art-house movies here: check www. cinemaclock.com for listings. There's also a huge range of movie festivals, including late-September's **Vancouver International Film Festival** (www.viff.org) and smaller fests such as May's **DOXA Documentary Film Festival** (www.doxafestival. ca) and November's **Vancouver Asian Film Festival** (www.vaff.org).

JANINES / SHUTTERSTOCK ©

Best Live Music Bars

Guilt & Co Subterranean bar with regular shows. (p70)

Railway Stage & Beer Cafe A small stage plus a great craft beer selection. (p50)

Uva Wine & Cocktail Bar Check ahead for live jazz nights. (p50)

Best Live Theater

Bard on the Beach Shakespeare plays performed in waterfront Vanier Park tents. (p144)

Theatre Under the Stars Summertime musical performances in Stanley Park. (p51)

Stanley Theatre Historic Arts Club theater venue with great end-of-season musicals. (pictured above left; p127)

Firehall Arts Centre Leading independent theater with eclectic lineup of shows. (p74)

Best Alternative Entertainment

Kino Flamenco performances several nights a week on a small stage. (p127)

Cinematheque Summer's film noir series at this beloved art-house cinema. (p51)

Rickshaw Theatre Under-the-radar thrash and punk venue. (p74)

What's on in Vancouver

○ Pick up Thursday's freebie *Georgia Straight* (www.straight.com) for what's on in the week ahead.

○ Head online to Live Van (www.livevan.com) for up-to-the-minute local gig listings.

For Kids

Family-friendly Vancouver is stuffed with activities and attractions for kids, including interactive science centers, animal encounters and plenty of outdoor activities to tire them out before bed. Several festivals are especially kid-tastic, and local transport experiences, including SeaBus and SkyTrain, are highlights for many youngsters.

DAN BRECKWOLDT / SHUTTERSTOCK © ARCHITECT BRUNO FRESCHI

Science & Nature

From space and science centers to outdoor attractions that illuminate the region's flora and fauna, Vancouver has lots of options for suitably inclined youngsters. Save time to hit the local trails: Stanley Park is ideal for junior explorers keen to dive into the natural world.

History Huggers

If your children love their museums, Vancouver has several attractions with a kid-friendly vibe. Vanier Park houses three museums and there are additional heritage attractions around the city, from a full-size steam engine to a sports hall of fame.

Best Museums & Attractions

Science World A hands-on science center packed with activities. (pictured; p100)

HR MacMillan Space Centre Perfect destination for astronomically minded children. (p139)

Engine 374 Pavilion Historic steam engine on display in Yaletown (p86)

Best for Nature Fans

Beaty Biodiversity Museum Immersive natural history attraction at University of British Columbia. (p138)

Capilano Suspension Bridge Park River-crossing pedestrian suspension bridge in a dramatic forest setting. (p56)

Stanley Park Nature House Learn all about the park's flora and fauna; summer wildlife tours included. (p44)

Festivals

While July and August are peak months for festivals, Vancouver has a year-round roster of events and happenings worth checking into before you arrive. Do your homework via the websites of local listings magazines such as the Georgia Straight *(www.straight.com) to see what's coming up.*

CDRIN / SHUTTERSTOCK ©

Art & Music

Cultural festivals are hugely popular with Vancouverites, and there are stage, film and art festivals of all sizes here throughout the year. But it's the live music events that seem to really bring the party-loving locals together, including huge annual jazz and folk events that have been running in the city for years.

Community Events

If you truly want to connect with the locals, plan to be in the city for the July 1 **Canada Day** party when thousands flock to Canada Place for live music, flag-waving and a fireworks finale. There are also many grassroots festivals throughout the year, including colorful events staged by the Chinese, Italian, Greek and Japanese communities.

Best Art Festivals

Vancouver International Film Festival Huge annual showcase of movies from Canada and around the world. (p16)

Vancouver International Jazz Festival (www.coastaljazz.ca) Stages around the city, with hundreds of live shows. (pictured)

Vancouver Mural Festival Centered on Main St, a summertime street art extravaganza. (p104)

Best Community Festivals

Pacific National Exhibition Century-old summertime fair that lures thousands of locals. (p112)

Chinese New Year Chinatown party in January or February, street parade included.

Car Free Day Vancouver Communities across the city close their streets for live music and activities. (p108)

Active Vancouver

Vancouver's variety of outdoorsy activities is a huge hook: you can ski in the morning and hit the beach in the afternoon; hike or bike scenic forests; paddleboard the coastline; or kayak to your heart's content – and it will be content, with grand mountain views as your backdrop. There's also a full menu of spectator sports here.

MARC BRUXELLE / SHUTTERSTOCK ©

Cycling & Hiking

Vancouver is a cycle-friendly city with designated routes and a bike-share scheme. For maps and resources, see www. vancouver.ca/cycling. There's also an active mountain-biking scene on the North Shore; start your research via www. nsmba.ca. Hiking-wise, the region is striped with cool options; see www. vancouvertrails.com for ideas.

On the Water

It's hard to beat the joy of a sunset kayak around the coastline here. But hitting the water isn't only about paddling: there are also plenty of opportunities to surf, kiteboard and stand-up paddleboard. And there are several operators that can take you out to sea here.

Best Outdoor Action

Stanley Park Seawall Scenic walking, jogging and cycling trail. (pictured; p44)

Arbutus Greenway Walk, jog or bike the city's linear park, from Kitsilano to the Fraser River. (p145)

Best Spectator Sports

Vancouver Canucks City's fave NHL hockey passion. (p52)

Vancouver Whitecaps The city's Major League Soccer team. (p91)

Vancouver Canadians Nostalgic minor league baseball fun. (p127-8)

Museums & Galleries

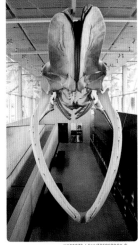

HASEG77 / SHUTTERSTOCK ©

While outdoor action monopolizes the spare time of many Vancouverites, there are also plenty of cultural attractions if you love rubbing your chin rather than your calves. Check to see what's on via local listings magazine the Georgia Straight (www.straight.com).

Museums

The city's de facto museum district, Vanier Park is home to three visit-worthy institutions, including Vancouver's main history museum. A short drive away, the University of British Columbia campus houses several excellent attractions, including a natural history museum and an anthropology-themed institution that many regard as Vancouver's best museum.

Galleries

Vancouver's main downtown art gallery is one of the finest in Western Canada. But the city is also home to several smaller art museums as well as a healthy array of private art galleries that always welcome visitors. Check the gallery websites for gallery show openings, exhibition dates and citywide art festivals.

Best Museums & Galleries

Museum of Anthropology Immersive UBC museum showcasing local First Nations as well as diverse global cultures. (p132)

Vancouver Art Gallery City's main gallery, with blockbuster visiting shows and local contemporary art. (p38)

Museum of Vancouver Telling the story of the region via several galleries. (p138)

Beaty Biodiversity Museum Natural history museum at UBC. (pictured; p138)

Engine 374 Pavilion Historic Vancouver steam locomotive, preserved in Yaletown (p86)

Under the Radar Vancouver

KARAMYSH / SHUTTERSTOCK ©

For those keen to encounter Vancouver beyond its well-known signature attractions, there are lots of walk-worthy neighborhoods, grassroots local experiences and off-the-beaten-path green spaces to discover.

Alternative Neighborhoods

Explore the independent shops and cafes on Main Street, the Victorian homes and heritage apartment buildings of the West End or the strollable storefronts and nearby beaches of Kitsilano's 4th Avenue area. From Kitsilano (pictured; p138), add a visit to the University of British Columbia (UBC) campus. This shoreline uni offers top-notch cultural attractions that are rarely crowded – don't miss the Museum of Anthropology (p132) or the Beaty Biodiversity Museum (p138).

Smaller Attractions

History buffs should visit the West End's Roedde House Museum (p44), downtown's art-deco Marine Building (p44) and Yaletown's free-entry Engine 374 Pavilion (p86) – home of the first transcontinental passenger train, which trundled into Vancouver in 1887. Need a nature break? Swap Stanley Park's (p44) crowded seawall promenade for its tranquil interior trails, complete with raccoons, hummingbirds and more. And if you're near downtown's Colosseum-shaped Vancouver Public Library (p45), nip inside and visit its 'secret' rooftop garden.

LGBTIQ+

ANTHONY BOWER / SHUTTERSTOCK ©

Vancouver's LGBTIQ+ scene is part of the city's culture rather than a sub-section of it. The legalization of same-sex marriage here makes it a popular spot for those who want to tie the knot in scenic style. But if you just want to kick back and have a good time, this is also Canada's top gay-friendly city.

West End

Sometimes called the Gay Village, the West End is the center of Vancouver's LGBTIQ+ scene, complete with pink-painted bus shelters and rainbow-striped street crossings. There's a full menu of scene-specific pubs and bars here, and it's a warm and welcoming district for everyone. Vancouver's Commercial Dr is also a traditional center of the lesbian scene. The city is highly gay-friendly, so you can expect lots of apposite events and happenings here.

Pride Week

Canada's biggest LGBTIQ+ celebration, Pride Week takes place in the first week of August. It's centered on a huge parade (pictured) of disco-pumping floats, drum-beating marching bands and barely clad locals dancing with boundless energy. There are also galas, drag contests, all-night parties and a popular queer film fest throughout the week. Around the same time, East Vancouver's annual Dyke March (www.vancouverdykemarch.com) also pops up, concluding with its own festival in Grandview Park.

Best Bars & Businesses

Fountainhead Pub Laid-back, beer-friendly gay community pub. (p50)

1181 Smooth lounge bar; great spot to see and be seen. (p50)

Little Sister's Book & Art Emporium Long-time 'gayborhood' legend, stocking books and beyond. (p53)

Four Perfect Days

Day 1

DEYMOSHR / SHUTTERSTOCK © ARCHITECT JOE Y WAI ARCHITECT INC.

Day 2

JOHN LEE / LONELY PLANET ©

Admire Gastown's **Maple Tree Square** on the site where Vancouver was founded, when Jack Deighton, a controversial figure in the city's early history, built a pub here. His nickname of Gassy Jack gave the surrounding area its name. Marvel at the square's handsome, late-19th-century houses, and browse the Water St shops, including **Herschel Supply** (p75) and **John Fluevog Shoes** (p75).

Chinatown, with its multicolored streets, is next door. Don't miss Pender St's **Chinatown Millennium Gate** (pictured; p67) and **Dr Sun Yat-Sen Classical Chinese Garden** (p62). Then sleuth out the **Vancouver Police Museum** (p60). Toast your day out by hopping bus 3 southwards along Main St to **Brassneck Brewery** (p106).

Explore the boutiques around the Main St and Broadway intersection, including vintage-fave **Mintage Mall** (pictured; p111) and arts and craft purveyors **Bird on a Wire** (p111). Then hop bus 3 southwards to the 18th Ave intersection.

Check out Vancouver's best indie stores, from vinyl-loving **Neptoon Records** (p111) to quirky **Regional Assembly of Text** (p110). Back on the bus, backtrack to the Broadway intersection and transfer to the 99B Line express, heading east to Commercial Dr.

Spend the evening on the Drive, one of Vancouver's best drink and dine 'hoods.

Day 3

RAINER PLENDL / SHUTTERSTOCK ©

Arrive early at **Stanley Park** (p34), strolling the **seawall** (p44), photographing the **totem poles** and nipping into the **Vancouver Aquarium** (pictured; p46). You'll also spot beady-eyed herons at **Lost Lagoon** – duck into the **Stanley Park Nature House** (p44) to find out more about them.

Depart the park for the tree-lined West End, including Davie and Denman Sts. Save time for **English Bay Beach** and **Roedde House Museum** (p44). Friendly coffee shops abound here.

The center of Vancouver's gay community, this area has plenty of inviting nightlife options for folks of all persuasions. Consider sunset-viewing cocktails at the charming **Sylvia's Bar & Lounge** (p49).

Day 4

MARTIN PATOCKA / SHUTTERSTOCK ©

Start your day at the University of British Columbia's **Museum of Anthropology** (p132) and **Beaty Biodiversity Museum**. Green-thumbed travellers should also add **UBC Botanical Garden** (p138) and **Nitobe Memorial Garden** (pictured; p139).

Then hop on bus 4 to Kitsilano's boutique-lined West 4th Ave. You'll find plenty of cool independent shops, cafes and restaurants, including **Zulu Records** (p145) and **49th Parallel Coffee** (p143-4).

Continue to Granville Island for craft beers at **Granville Island Brewing** (p87). Finally, catch an improv show at **Vancouver Theatresports** (p92; just remember: if you sit in the front, they'll likely pick on you).

Need to Know

For detailed information, see Survival Guide p147

Currency
Canadian dollar ($)

Language
English

Visas
Not required for US, Commonwealth and some European visitors. Required by those from 130 other countries. Most foreign nationals **flying** here require a **$7 Electronic Travel Authorization (eTA).** See www.canada.ca/eta for details. For visa information, visit the Canada Border Services Agency, visit the www.cbsa.gc.ca) website.

Mobile Phones
Local SIM cards may be used with some international phones. Check your provider's roaming charges.

Money
ATMs are widespread. Most businesses accept credit cards.

Time
Pacific Time (GMT/UTC minus eight hours)

Daily Budget

Budget: Less than $100
Dorm bed: $50
Food-court meal: $10; pizza slice: $3
Happy-hour beer special: $6
All-day transit pass: $10.25

Midrange: $100–$300
Double room in a standard hotel: $200
Dinner for two in a neighborhood restaurant: $40 (excluding drinks)
Craft beer for two: $15
Museum entry: $15–$25

Top End: More than $300
Four-star hotel room: from $350
Fine-dining meal for two: $100
Cocktails for two: $25
Taxi trips around the city: $5 and up

Advance Planning

Three months before Book summer-season hotel stays and sought-after tickets for hot shows, festivals and live performances.

One month before Book car rental and reserve a table at a top restaurant or two. Buy tickets for Vancouver Canucks and Vancouver Whitecaps games.

One week before Check the *Georgia Straight*'s online listings (www.straight.com) to see what local events are coming up.

Arriving in Vancouver

✈ Vancouver International Airport

YVR is 13km from downtown. To reach the city center, hop Canada Line SkyTrain services ($8-$10.75), take a taxi (around $35) or hire a car.

🚆 Pacific Central Station

Vancouver's long-distance train station is near the Main St-Science World SkyTrain transit station, a five-minute ride from downtown. Taxis are also available here.

⚓ BC Ferries

BC Ferries vessels from around the region dock at Tsawwassen, an hour south of Vancouver, and Horseshoe Bay, 30 minutes away in West Vancouver. Both are linked to transit bus services.

Getting Around

🚲 Bicycle

Vancouver has 300km of designated bike routes and a public bike share scheme.

⚓ Boat

Local miniferries and public transit Sea-Buses navigate city waterways.

🚌 Bus

Extensive TransLink public bus services operate in Vancouver and beyond.

🚆 Train

TransLink's rapid-transit SkyTrains service local and suburban destinations.

🚕 Taxi

Several taxi companies operate here. Ride-share services were being introduced at time of research.

Gastown (p59)

BARRY WINIKER / GETTY IMAGES ©

Vancouver Neighborhoods

Yaletown & Granville Island (p77)

On opposite sides of False Creek, these enticing areas host some of the city's best shopping and dining options.

◉ *Museum of Anthropology*

Kitsilano & University of British Columbia (p131)

Beaches and heritage homes lure the locals to Kits while the nearby campus has some top day-out attractions.

Capilano Suspension
Bridge Park ◉

Downtown & West End (p33)

Lined with shops and restaurants, city center Vancouver adjoins the largely reidential West End plus spectacular Stanley Park.

Gastown & Chinatown (p59)

Side-by-side historic neighborhoods studded with some of Vancouver's best bars, restaurants and one-of-a-kind boutiques.

Stanley Park ◉

Vancouver Art Gallery ◉

Vancouver Police Museum ◉

◉

Granville Island Public Market ◉

◉ *Science World*

— *Dr Sun Yat-Sen Classical Chinese Garden*

Main Street (p99)

The skinny-jeaned heart of Vancouver's hipster scene houses many of its best independent cafes, shops and restaurants.

VanDusen Botanical Garden ◉

Fairview & South Granville (p115)

Twin residential areas with highly walkable shopping and dining streets plus some green attractions.

Explore
Vancouver

Worth a Trip 👀

Vancouver's Walking Tours 🥾

Downtown (p33) MATTEO COLOMBO / GETTY IMAGES ©

Explore

Downtown & West End

The heart of Vancouver is an ocean-fringed peninsula easily divided into three: the grid-pattern city center streets of shops, restaurants and glass towers fanning from the intersection of Granville and West Georgia Sts; the well-maintained 1950s apartment blocks and residential side streets of the West End (also home to Vancouver's gay district); and Stanley Park, Canada's finest urban green space.

The Short List

○ **Stanley Park Seawall (p44)** *Strolling or cycling the perimeter pathway for sigh-triggering views of the forest-fringed ocean.*

○ **Marine Building (p44)** *Spotting multiple ocean- and transport-themed motifs on the exterior of this art-deco skyscraper masterpiece.*

○ **Roedde House Museum (p44)** *Nosing around antique-lined rooms at this handsome heritage home, an evocative reminder of yesteryear Vancouver.*

Getting There & Around

🚶 Downtown's grid street system is walkable and easy to navigate.

🚆 SkyTrain's Expo Line and Canada Line both run through downtown.

🚌 Bus 5 trundles along Robson St, bus 6 along Davie St, bus 10 along Granville St and bus 19 into Stanley Park.

🚗 There are multiple car parks and parking meters here. Stanley Park has pay-and-display parking.

Downtown & West End Map on p42

Top Experience 📷
Walk the Stanley Park Seawall

One of North America's largest urban green spaces, Stanley Park is revered for its dramatic forest-and-mountain oceanfront views. But there's more to this 400-hectare woodland than looks. The park is studded with nature-hugging trails, family-friendly attractions, sunset-loving beaches and tasty places to eat. There's also the occasional unexpected sight to search for (besides the raccoons that call the place home).

◎ **MAP P42, C1**

www.vancouver.ca/parks

🅿 🚻

🚌 19

Seawall

Built in stages between 1917 and 1980, the park's 8.8km **seawall** trail is Vancouver's favorite outdoor hangout. Encircling the park, it offers spectacular waterfront vistas on one side and dense forest on the other. You can walk the whole thing in roughly three hours or rent a bike to cover the route far faster. Keep in mind: cyclists and in-line skaters must travel counterclockwise on the seawall, so there's no going back once you start your trundle (unless you walk).

The seawall delivers you to some of the park's top highlights. About 1.5km from the W Georgia St entrance, you'll come to the ever-popular **totem poles** (pictured). Remnants of an abandoned 1930s plan to create a First Nations 'theme village,' the bright-painted poles were joined by some exquisitely carved Coast Salish welcome arches. For the full First Nations story, consider a fascinating guided park walk with Talaysay Tours (www.talaysay.com).

Natural Attractions

Stanley Park is studded with appeal for wildlife fans. Start at **Lost Lagoon**, a beloved nature sanctuary near the W Georgia St entrance. On its perimeter pathway, keep your eyes peeled for blue herons and a wandering raccoon or two. Plunging deeper into the park's more secluded trails, you'll also likely spot wrens, hummingbirds and chittering Douglas squirrels. And while they mostly give humans a wide berth, you might also come across a coyote or two; treat them with respect and give them a wide berth as well. For an introduction to the area's flora and fauna, start at the Stanley Park Nature House (p44). You'll find friendly volunteers and exhibits on wildlife, history and ecology – ask about their well-priced guided walks.

★ Top Tips

o It takes around three hours to walk the 8.8km Stanley Park seawall; bike rentals are also available on nearby Denman St.

o In summer, the seawall is packed; arrive early morning or early evening instead.

o Sidestep the Vancouver Aquarium's summer queues by making it your first stop of the day.

o Gather together a great picnic and snag a grassy spot near Lumberman's Arch.

✖ Take a Break

The handsomely renovated Prospect Point Bar & Grill (p49) is a great spot for patio feasting; through the trees you'll see the Lions Gate Bridge.

Dining options abound on nearby Denman St and Robson St; consider slow-cooked salmon at Forage (p48).

Beaches & Views

If it's sandy beaches you're after, the park has several alluring options. **Second Beach** is a family-friendly area on the park's western side, with a grassy playground, an ice-cream-serving concession and a huge outdoor swimming **pool**. It's also close to **Ceperley Meadows**, where popular free outdoor movie screenings are staged in summer. But for a little more tranquility, try **Third Beach**. A sandy expanse with plenty of logs to sit against, this is a favored summer-evening destination for Vancouverites.

There's a plethora of additional vistas in the park, but perhaps the most popular is at **Prospect Point.** One of Vancouver's best lookouts, this lofty spot is located at the park's northern tip. In summer you'll be jostling for elbow room

with tour parties; heading down the steep stairs to the viewing platform usually shakes them off. The area's revitalized Prospect Point Bar & Grill (p49) offers refreshments – aim for a deck table.

Statue Spotting

Stanley Park is studded with statues, all of which come to life at night (just kidding). On your leisurely amble around the tree-lined idyll, look out for the following and award yourself 10 points for each one you find. If you're on the seawall, it shouldn't be hard to spot *Girl in a Wetsuit*, a 1972 bronze by Elek Imredy that sits in the water. But how about the Robbie Burns statue unveiled by British prime minister Ramsay MacDonald in 1928 or the dramatic bronze of Canadian sprint legend Harry

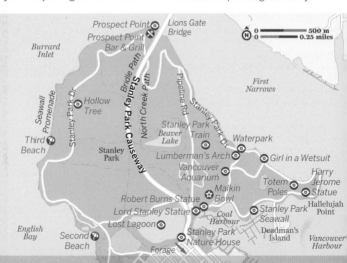

The Poet of Stanley Park

The only person to be legally buried in Stanley Park is writer Pauline Johnson. A champion of First Nations culture, her book on Coast Salish legends was a bestseller. When she died in 1913, thousands of locals lined the streets to mark her passing. Her memorial is a few steps from the seawall's Siwash Rock landmark.

Jerome, who held six world records and won a bronze at the 1964 Summer Olympics? Here's a clue for the next one: it's near **Malkin Bowl.** Marking the first official visit to Canada by a US president, this elegant statue is actually a memorial: after visiting in 1923, Warren Harding died a week later in San Francisco.

For Kids

It doesn't take much to plan an entire day with children here. As well as the aquarium and the Nature House, there are some additional must-dos for under-10s. Beeline to the waterfront **waterpark** near Lumberman's Arch; there's also a playground here. Dry the kids off with a trundle on the **Stanley Park Train.** Near the aquarium, this replica of the first passenger train that rolled into Vancouver in 1887 is a family favorite.

Before leaving the park, visit the man behind the fun day you've just had. Take the ramp running parallel with the seawall near the W Georgia St entrance and you'll find an almost-hidden **statue of Lord Stanley** with his arms outstretched, nestled in the trees. On his plinth are the words he used at the park's 1889 dedication ceremony: 'To the use and enjoyment of people of all colours, creeds and customs for all time.' It's a sentiment that still resonates loudly here today.

The Hollow Tree

In its early tourist destination days, a giant western red cedar was the park's top attraction. The tree's bottom section had a massive hollowed-out area where visitors would pose for photos, sometimes in their cars. The fragile structure still remains, while artist Douglas Coupland has celebrated it with a latter-day golden replica near the city's Marine Drive Canada Line station.

Top Experience

Dress Up for a Vancouver Art Gallery Social Evening

Residing in a heritage courthouse building but inching toward opening a fancy new venue, the Vancouver Art Gallery (VAG) is the region's most important art gallery. It's also a vital part of the city's cultural scene. Contemporary exhibitions – often showcasing the Vancouver School of renowned photoconceptualists – are combined with global blockbuster traveling shows.

MAP P42, F5

604-662-4700

www.vanartgallery.bc.ca

750 Hornby St, Downtown

adult/child $24/6.50

10am-5pm Wed-Mon, to 9pm Tue

5

VAG 101

Before you arrive at the VAG, check online for details of the latest exhibitions; the biggest shows of the year are typically in summer. But the VAG isn't just about blockbusters. If you have time, explore this landmark gallery's other offerings. Start on the top floor, where British Columbia's most famous painter is often show-cased. Emily Carr (1871–1945) is celebrated for her swirling, nature-inspired paintings of regional landscapes and First Nations culture. Watercolors were her main approach, and the gallery has a large collection of her works.

Join the Locals

The gallery isn't just a place to geek out over cool art. In fact, locals treat it as an important part of their social calendar. Every few months, the VAG stages its regular **FUSE** socials, which transform the domed heritage venue into a highly popular evening event with DJs, bars, live performances and quirky gallery tours. Vancou-verites dress up and treat the event as one of the highlights of the city's art scene; expect a clubby vibe to pervade proceedings.

Offsite

Three blocks from the VAG on W Georgia St – in the shadow of the monolithic Shangri-La Hotel – **Offsite** is the gallery's small, somewhat incongruous, but always thought-provoking outdoor installation space. The alfresco con-temporary works here are changed twice yearly and they routinely inspire passersby to whip out their camera phones for an impromptu snap or two. The installations have varied wildly over the years but have included gigantic photo portraits of Chinese children and scale models of local cannery buildings.

★ Top Tips

o On Tuesdays, be-tween 5pm and 9pm, entry is by donation.

o Seniors can also partake of entry by donation on the first Monday of every month between 10am and 1pm.

o Check the VAG's online calendar for curator talks and ex-pert lectures; online registration is typi-cally recommended.

✖ Take a Break

The large patio of the on-site **Gallery Café** (☎604-688-2233; www.thegallery cafe.ca; mains $7-12; ⏰9am-6pm Wed-Mon, to 9pm Tue; 🛜) is a great spot to grab a coffee and people-watch over bustling Robson St.

For a fancy dinner to conclude your artsy day out, chic Hawks-worth (p49) is just a few steps away.

Walking Tour 🥾

Downtown Grand Tour

The heart of city centre Vancouver is a grid of major streets lined with shops and restaurants. But it's also home to galleries, historic buildings and an accessible rooftop garden that overlooks downtown's shimmering glass towers. Follow the route below and take your time; you'll find plenty of pit-stop cafes and coffee shops en route.

Walk Facts

Start Olympic Cauldron
End Marine Building
Length 3km; one hour

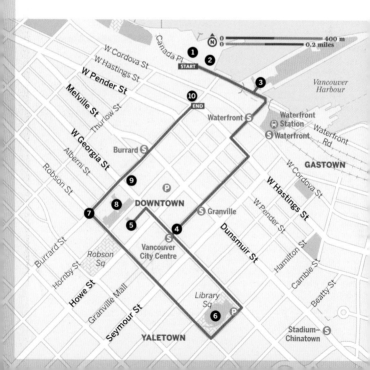

❶ Olympic Cauldron

A landmark reminder of Vancouver's 2010 Olympic Winter Games, check out the tripod-like Olympic Cauldron. Only occasionally lit these days, it's a great spot for photos with a grand mountain backdrop.

❷ Convention Centre

The adjacent Convention Centre West Building hugs the waterfront. Follow its external walkway for some giant public artworks, including a pixelated Orca and a bright blue raindrop.

❸ Canada Place

The area's original convention centre building, sail-shaped Canada Place (p45) is next door. Stroll its pier-like outer promenade and watch the floatplanes taking off and landing on the water.

❹ Granville & Georgia Sts

Swap the scenic waterfront for downtown's bustling thoroughfares. You'll pass shops and cafes before reaching the ever-busy intersection of Granville & Georgia Sts.

❺ Vancouver Art Gallery

Inside a stately heritage building, the Vancouver Art Gallery (p38) is a must-do (especially the top floor Emily Carr paintings). Ravenously hungry? Dive into the nearby food trucks for an alfresco lunch.

❻ Vancouver Public Library

There's much more than books to check out at the Colosseum-like Vancouver Public Library (p45). Press floor nine in the elevator to reach a large public garden with cityscape views.

❼ Robson & Burrard Sts

Consider your dinner options around the intersection of Robson and Burrard Sts. You'll find a tempting menu of possibilities, from spicy Thai to pub grub.

❽ Fairmont Hotel

The city's grand-dame heritage sleepover, nip into the lobby of the Fairmont Hotel Vancouver. Look for 1930s design features and the two friendly dogs that call the concierge desk home.

❾ Christ Church Cathedral

Historic Christ Church Cathedral (p46) seems incongruous among the glass towers. Gaze at its stained glass windows and eye-popping hammerbeam ceiling.

❿ Marine Building

The spectacular Marine Building (p44) was completed during the height of the art deco era. Give yourself plenty of time to peruse its exterior transport and maritime-themed decorative flourishes, then nip inside and gawk at its palatial lobby.

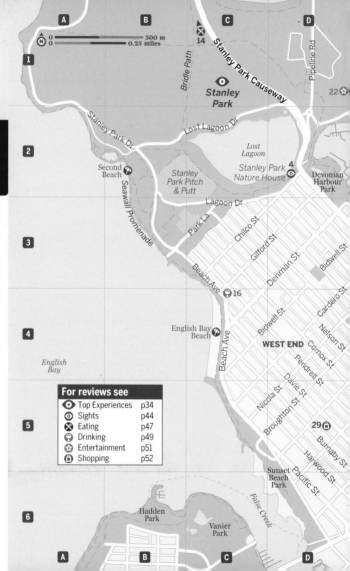

A **B** **C** **D**

0 ──────── 500 m
0 ──────── 0.25 miles

1

Bridle Path

✕ 14

Stanley Park Causeway

Pipeline Rd

22 ☆

Stanley Park

Stanley Park Dr

Lost Lagoon Dr

Lost Lagoon

2

Second Beach

Seawall Promenade

Stanley Park Pitch & Putt

Stanley Park Nature House

4

Devonian Harbour Park

Lagoon Dr

Park La

Chilco St

Gilford St

Denman St

Bidwell St

3

Beach Ave

16

Bidwell St

Cardero St

Nelson St

4

English Bay Beach

English Bay

Beach Ave

WEST END

Comox St

Pendrell St

Davie St

Nicola St

Broughton St

Burnaby St

For reviews see

◉	Top Experiences	p34
◉	Sights	p44
✕	Eating	p47
🍷	Drinking	p49
☆	Entertainment	p51
🔒	Shopping	p52

5

29 🔒

Harwood St

Sunset Beach Park

Pacific St

False Creek

6

Hadden Park

Vanier Park

A **B** **C** **D**

E　　F　　G　　H

1

Brockton
Point

Seawall Promenade

8 Vancouver
Aquarium

Brockton
Oval

Stanley Park
Seawall

2

Stanley Park Dr

Hallelujah
Point

2

Coal
Harbour

Deadman's
Island

HMCS Discovery
Naval Training
Station

Vancouver
Harbour

Royal
Vancouver
Yacht Club

Bayshore Dr

3

Coal Harbour Seawall

Coal
Harbour
Park

Harbour
Green Park

Tourism
Vancouver
Visitor
Centre

W Cordova St

Canada Pl

Canada
Place

5

Nicola St

Broughton St

Jervis St

W Pender St

Melville St

W Hastings St

Marine
Building

3

30 Waterfront

Waterfront Rd

4

Barclay
Heritage
Sq
1

12

W Georgia St

Alberni St

Vancouver Bullion
& Currency Exchange

Waterfront
Station

Roedde House
Museum

Robson St

Haro St

Burrard

Christ
Church 7
Cathedral

DOWNTOWN

17

W Cordova St

Bute St

Barclay St

Thurlow St

Nelson
Park

9

15

Cycle City
Tours

Granville

10

W Hastings St

5

21

Burrard St

Hornby St

Vancouver
Art Gallery

Robson
Sq

Sky Train
Canada Line

18

Vancouver
City Centre

26
28

11

W Pender St

Dunsmuir St

SkyTrain

13

20

Howe St

Helmcken St

23

Davie St

Granville St

27

24

Seymour St

19

Robson St

Smithe St

S Richards St

S Homer St

Vancouver
Public
Library

6

Hamilton St

Cambie St

Stadium–
Chinatown

25

6

Griffiths Way

Drake St

Nelson St

Beatty St

YALETOWN

BC Place
Stadium

E　　F　　G　　H

Sights

Roedde House Museum

MUSEUM

1 ◎ MAP P42, E4

For a glimpse of what the West End looked like before the apartment blocks, visit this handsome 1893 Queen Anne–style mansion, now a lovingly preserved museum. Designed by infamous architect Francis Rattenbury, the yesteryear, antique-studded rooms have a lived-in feel while its guided tour (included with admission) tells you all about its middle-class Roedde family residents. Look out for the cylinder record player, 250-year-old grandfather clock and the taxidermied heads of deer that were hunted in Stanley Park in 1906. (☏604-684-7040; www.roeddehouse.org; 1415 Barclay St, West End; $5, Sun $8; ⏱1-4pm Tue-Fri & Sun; ☒5)

Stanley Park Seawall

WATERFRONT

2 ◎ MAP P42, E2

Built between 1917 and 1980, the 8.8km seawall trail (p34) is Vancouver's favorite outdoor hangout. Encircling the whole of Stanley Park, it offers breathtaking waterfront, mountain-fringed vistas on one side and dense forest canopy on the other. You can walk the whole thing in around three blister-triggering hours or rent a bike from the Denman St operators near the park entrance to cover the route faster. But what's the rush? Slow down and slide into the natural side of life instead. (Stanley Park; ☒19)

Marine Building

HISTORIC BUILDING

3 ◎ MAP P42, G4

Vancouver's most romantic old-school tower block, and also its best art-deco building, the elegant 22-story Marine Building is a tribute to the city's maritime past. Check out its elaborate exterior of seahorses, lobsters and streamlined steamships, then nip into the lobby, which is like a walk-through artwork. Stained-glass panels and a polished floor inlaid with signs of the zodiac await. (355 Burrard St, Downtown; ⓢBurrard)

Stanley Park Nature House

NATURE RESERVE

4 ◎ MAP P42, D2

Illuminating the breathtaking array of flora and fauna just steps from the busy streets of the West End, this charming nature center is a great introduction to Stanley Park's wild side. The chatty volunteers will tell you all you need to know about the area's critters, from coyotes to Douglas squirrels and from blue herons to black-capped chickadees. Guided nature walks are also offered or you can wander the park's trails on your own armed with your new-found wildlife expertise. (☏604-257-8544; www.stanleyparkecology.ca; north end of Alberni St, Lost Lagoon, Stanley Park; admission free; ⏱10am-5pm Tue-Sun Jul & Aug, 10am-4pm Sat & Sun Sep-Jun; ♿; ☒19)

Canada Place

LANDMARK

5  MAP P42, H4

Vancouver's version of the Sydney Opera House – judging by the number of postcards it appears on – this iconic landmark is shaped like sails jutting into the sky over the harbor. Both a cruise-ship terminal and a convention center, it's also a stroll-worthy pier, providing photogenic views of the busy floatplane action and looming North Shore mountains. Here for Canada Day on July 1? This is the center of the city's festivities, with displays, live music and a finale fireworks display. (604-665-9000; www.canadaplace.ca; 999 Canada Place Way, Downtown; admission free; P; S Waterfront)

Vancouver Public Library

LIBRARY

6  MAP P42, G6

This dramatic Colosseum-like building must be a temple to the great god of libraries. If not, it's certainly one of the world's most magnificent book-lending facilities. Designed by Moshe Safdie and opened in 1995, its collections (including lendable musical instruments) are arranged over several floors. Head straight up to floor nine for the **Rooftop Garden**, a lofty, tree-lined outdoor plaza lined with tables and chairs. (604-331-3603; www.vpl.ca; 350 W Georgia St, Downtown; 10am-9pm Mon-Thu, to 6pm Fri & Sat, 11am-6pm Sun; P; S Stadium-Chinatown)

Downtown & West End Sights

Marine Building

JOHN LEE / LONELY PLANET ©

Vancouver's Favorite Public Artwork

Head toward the West End's English Bay Beach and you'll be stopped in your tracks by 14 very tall men. *A-maze-ing Laughter* by Yue Minjun comprises a gathering of oversized bronze figures permanently engaged in a hearty round of chuckling – a permanent artwork legacy from the city's **Vancouver Biennale** (www.vancouverbiennale.com). Check the website for additional artsy installations.

Christ Church Cathedral
CATHEDRAL

7 ⊙ MAP P42, F4

Completed in 1895 and designated as a cathedral in 1929, the city's most attractive Gothic-style church is nestled incongruously alongside looming glass towers. When services aren't being held, casual visitors are warmly welcomed: check out the dramatic hammerbeam wooden ceiling plus the slender glass-encased bell tower that was more recently added to the exterior. The cathedral is also home to a wide range of cultural events, including regular choir and chamber music recitals and the occasional Shakespeare reading. (☏604-682-3848; www.thecathedral.ca; 690 Burrard St, Downtown; admission free; ⊙10am-4pm Mon-Fri; Ⓢ Burrard)

Vancouver Aquarium
AQUARIUM

8 ⊙ MAP P42, E1

Stanley Park's biggest draw is home to 9000 critters – including sharks, wolf eels and a somewhat shy octopus. There's also a small, walk-through rainforest area of birds, turtles and a statue-still sloth. The aquarium keeps captive whales and dolphins and organizes animal encounters with these and its other creatures, which may concern some visitors. (☏604-659-3400; www.vanaqua.org; 845 Avison Way, Stanley Park; adult/child $38/21; ⊙9:30am-6pm Jul & Aug, 10am-5pm Sep-Jun; ♿; ☐19)

Cycle City Tours
CYCLING

9 ⊙ MAP P42, G5

Striped with bike lanes, Vancouver is a good city for two-wheeled exploring. But if you're not great at navigating, consider a guided tour with this popular operator. Its Grand Tour ($90) is a great city intro, while its Craft Beer Tour ($90) includes brunch and three breweries. Alternatively, go solo with a rental; there's a bike lane outside the store. (☏604-618-8626; www.cyclevancouver.com; 648 Hornby St, Downtown; tours from $65, bicycle rentals per hour/day $9.50/38; ⊙9am-6pm, reduced hours in winter; Ⓢ Burrard)

Eating

Poke Guy

HAWAIIAN $

10  MAP P42, H5

Trip down the steps (not literally) to this busy Vancouver eating spot and you'll find one of the city's favorite *poke* bowl destinations. Expect to find friendly service, heaped bowls of fresh, quality ingredients and a choice of set menu options (the salmon belly *lomi lomi* is highly recommended) or build-your-own bowls, all available in two sizes. The food here is good value: you will feel fully fortified for your downtown on-foot exploration. (778-379-8455; www.thepokeguy. ca; 420 Richards St, Downtown; mains

$9-14; 11am-7pm Mon-Fri, 11:30am-6pm Sat; 14)

Finch's

CAFE $

11 MAP P42, H5

For a coveted seat at one of the dinged old tables, arrive off-peak at this sunny, superfriendly corner cafe, which combines creaky wooden floors and a junk-shop bric-a-brac aesthetic. Join hipsters and office workers who've been calling this their local for years and who come mainly for the freshly prepared baguette sandwiches (pear, blue Brie, prosciutto and roasted walnuts recommended). (604-899-4040; www.finchtea house.com; 353 W Pender St, Downtown; mains $6-12; 9am-5pm Mon-Fri, 11am-4pm Sat; 4)

Downtown has top spots for sustenance and craft beer

TRACEY KUSIEWICZ/FOODIE PHOTOGRAPHY / GETTY IMAGES ©

Forage

CANADIAN $$

12 MAP P42, E4

A popular farm-to-table eatery, this sustainability-focused restaurant is the perfect way to sample regional flavors. Brunch has become a firm local favorite (halibut eggs benny recommended), and for dinner there's everything from bison steaks to slow-cooked salmon. Add a flight of British Columbia (BC) craft beers, with top choices from the likes of Four Winds, Strange Fellows and more. Reservations recommended. (604-661-1400; www.foragevancouver.com; 1300 Robson St, West End; mains $16-35; 6:30-10am & 5-11pm Mon-Fri, 7am-2pm & 5-11pm Sat & Sun; ; 5)

Jam Cafe

BREAKFAST $$

13 MAP P42, H5

The Vancouver outpost of Victoria's wildly popular breakfast and brunch superstar lures the city's longest lineups, especially on weekends. Reservations are not accepted so you're well advised to dine off-peak and during the week. You'll find a white-walled room studded with Canadian knickknacks and a huge array of satisfying options, from chicken and biscuits to red-velvet pancakes. (778-379-1992; www.jamcafes.com; 556 Beatty St, Downtown; mains $9-17; 8am-3pm; ; S Stadium-Chinatown)

Hawksworth

JENNIFER JESSICA PECK / SHUTTERSTOCK ©

Prospect Point Bar & Grill

CANADIAN $$

14 MAP P42, C1

A sparkling renovation has transformed this historic wood-beamed cafe into a full-service bistro and bar serving elevated comfort food from burgers to *poke* bowls and panko-crusted fish and chips. You'll also find BC craft beers: perfect for toasting your luck at finding one of the city's best patios, a tree-framed treasure overlooking the grand Lions Gate Bridge. (604-669-2737; www.prospectpoint.com; 5601 Stanley Park Dr, Stanley Park; mains $16-24; 9am-7pm, reduced hours off-season; 19)

Hawksworth

NORTHWESTERN US $$$

15 MAP P42, G5

The fine-dining anchor of the top-end Rosewood Hotel Georgia is a see-and-be-seen spot for swank dates and business meetings. Created by and named after one of Vancouver's top chefs, its menu fuses contemporary West Coast approaches with clever international influences, hence dishes such as ling cod with orange lassi. There's also a *prix fixe* lunch ($28). (604-673-7000; www.hawksworthrestaurant.com; 801 W Georgia St, Downtown; mains $38-58; 7am-11pm; P ; S Vancouver City Centre)

Local Dining

Restaurants on Robson St are always lined with tourists, but locals are much more likely to be dining out at the better-priced neighborhood eateries on Denman and Davie Sts in the West End, including Japanese, Spanish and Indian options.

Drinking

Sylvia's Bar & Lounge

BAR

16 MAP P42, C4

Part of the permanently popular Sylvia Hotel, this was Vancouver's first cocktail bar when it opened in the mid-1950s. Now a comfy, wood-lined neighborhood bar favored by in-the-know locals (they're the ones hogging the window seats as the sun sets over English Bay), it's a charming spot for an end-of-day wind down. There's live music on Wednesdays, Thursdays and Sundays. (604-681-9321; www.sylviahotel.com; 1154 Gilford St, West End; 7am-11pm Sun-Thu, to midnight Fri & Sat; 5)

Mario's Coffee Express

COFFEE

17 MAP P42, G4

A java-lover's favorite that only downtown office workers seem to know about. You'll wake up and smell the coffee long before you make it through the door here. The rich aromatic brews served up by the man himself are the kind of ambrosia that makes Starbucks' drinkers weep. You might even forgive the 1980s Italian pop percolating through the shop. (📞604-608-2804; www.facebook.com/marioscoffeeexpress; 595 Howe St, Downtown; ⏱6:30am-4pm Mon-Fri; 🚇Burrard)

Railway Stage & Beer Cafe
BAR

18 🚇 MAP P42, G5

The near-legendary former Railway Club has been recreated as a scrubbed-up version of its belovedly grungy original incarnation. There are still regular live performances held here, especially on weekends, while the expanded draft beer menu covers an ever-changing array of British Columbia brews; Hoyne Dark Matter recommended. Sandwiches and salad bowls keep the serving hatch busy and the communal long tables full. (📞604-564-1430; www.facebook.com/RailwaySBC; 579 Dunsmuir St, Downtown; ⏱4pm-2am Sun-Thu, 11am-3am Fri & Sat; 📶; 🚇Granville)

Uva Wine & Cocktail Bar
LOUNGE

19 🚇 MAP P42, F6

This sexy nook fuses a heritage mosaic floor with a dash of mod class. Despite the cool appearances, there's a snob-free approach that encourages taste-tripping through an extensive by-the-glass wine menu and some dangerously delicious cocktails – we love the Diplomat. Food is part of the mix (including shareable small plates) and there's a daily 2pm to 5pm happy hour. (📞604-632-9560; www.uvavancouver.com; 900 Seymour St, Downtown; ⏱2pm-2am; 📶; 🚌10)

Fountainhead Pub
GAY

20 🚇 MAP P42, E6

The area's loudest and proudest gay neighborhood pub, this friendly joint is all about the patio, which spills onto Davie St. Take part in the ongoing summer-evening pastime of ogling passersby or retreat to a quieter spot inside for a few lagers or a naughty cocktail: anyone for a Crispy Crotch or a Slippery Nipple? (📞604-687-2222; www.fthdpub.com; 1025 Davie St, West End; ⏱11am-midnight Mon-Thu & Sun, to 2am Fri & Sat; 🚌6)

1181
GAY

21 🚇 MAP P42, E5

This intimate Davie St 'gayborhood' mainstay is a loungey, two-room late-night hangout where flirty cocktails rule. Check ahead for events and happenings but expect a wide array of options from drag nights to improv comedy to DJ dance parties. This is the area's classiest gay bar. (www.facebook.com/1181Lounge; 1181 Davie St, West End; ⏱7pm-3am; 🚌6)

Citizen of the Century

Born in Trinidad in 1863, **Joe Fortes** arrived in Vancouver in 1885, when only a few hundred African American men lived in the fledgling townsite. Reputedly saving a mother and child during the area's 1886 Great Fire, he later settled around English Bay in the West End. From here, he became a self-appointed lifeguard, saving dozens of lives and teaching thousands of children to swim over the years. The city made him its first official lifeguard in 1897, presenting him with a gold watch for devoted service in 1910. When he died in 1922, his funeral was one of the biggest in Vancouver. Fortes' memory lives on: a city restaurant and a public library are named after him, Canada Post released a stamp depicting him in 2013, and the Vancouver Historical Society named him 'Citizen of the Century' in 1986.

Entertainment

Theatre under the Stars

PERFORMING ARTS

22 MAP P42, D1

The charming **Malkin Bowl** (www. malkinbowl.com; 610 Pipeline Rd, Stanley Park; 19) provides an atmospheric alfresco stage for the summertime TUTS season, usually featuring two interchanging Broadway musicals. It's hard to find a better place to catch a show, especially as the sun fades over the surrounding Stanley Park (p34) trees. The troupe's production values have massively increased over the years, and these productions are slick, professional and energetic. (TUTS; 604-631-2877; www.tuts.ca; tickets from $30; Jul & Aug)

Cinematheque

CINEMA

23 MAP P42, E6

This beloved cinema operates like an ongoing film festival with a daily-changing program of movies. A $3 annual membership is required – organize it at the door – before you can skulk in the dark with other chin-stroking movie buffs who probably named their children (or pets) after Fellini and Bergman. (604-688-8202; www.thecinema theque.ca; 1131 Howe St, Downtown; tickets $12, double bills $16; 10)

Commodore Ballroom

LIVE MUSIC

24 MAP P42, F5

Local bands know they've made it when they play Vancouver's best midsized venue, a restored art-deco ballroom that still has the city's bounciest dance floor –

Urban Birding

Birding has become a popular pastime for many Vancouverites and if you're keen to join in the feather-fancying fun, head to **Stanley Park** (p34), **Vanier Park**, **Pacific Spirit Park** or **Queen Elizabeth Park**. Many city streets are also home to a diverse array of beak-tastic critters: on our West End exploration, we spotted hummingbirds, barred owls and northern flicker woodpeckers. Heading into adjoining Stanley Park, you might also see bald eagles, cormorants and herons – which are also famous for nesting in a large and noisy heronry here every spring.

courtesy of tires placed under its floorboards. If you need a break from moshing, collapse at one of the tables lining the perimeter, catch your breath with a bottled brew and then plunge back in. (☎604-739-4550; www.commodoreballroom.com; 868 Granville St, Downtown; tickets from $30; 🚍10)

Vancouver Canucks HOCKEY

25 ✪ MAP P42, H6

Recent years haven't been hugely successful for Vancouver's National Hockey League (NHL) team, which means it's sometimes easy to snag tickets to a game if you're simply visiting and want to see what 'ice hockey' (no one calls it that here) is all about. You'll hear 'go Canucks, go!' booming from the seats and in local bars on game nights. (☎604-899-7400; www.nhl.com/canucks; 800 Griffiths Way, Rogers Arena, Downtown; tickets from $47; 🕙Sep-Apr; Ⓢ Stadium-Chinatown)

Shopping

Paper Hound BOOKS

26 🔒 MAP P42, H5

Proving the printed word is alive and kicking, this small but perfectly curated secondhand bookstore is a dog-eared favorite among locals. A perfect spot for browsing, you'll find tempting tomes (mostly used but some new) on everything from nature to poetry to chaos theory. Ask for recommendations; they really know their stuff here. Don't miss the bargain rack out front. (☎604-428-1344; www.paper hound.ca; 344 W Pender St, Downtown; 🕙10am-7pm Sun-Thu, to 8pm Fri & Sat; 🚍14)

Golden Age Collectables BOOKS

27 🔒 MAP P42, F5

If you're missing your regular dose of *Hulkverines* or you just want to blow your vacation budget on a highly detailed life-sized model of Conan the Barbarian, head

FARTS PFOTOGRAFY / SHUTTERSTOCK ©

Mink Chocolates

straight to this Aladdin's cave of the comic-book world. While the clientele is unsurprisingly dominated by males, the staff are friendly and welcoming – especially to wide-eyed kids buying their first *Amazing Spider-Man*. (☎604-683-2819; www.gacvan.com; 852 Granville St, Downtown; ⌚10am-9pm Mon-Sat, 11am-6pm Sun; 🚌10)

Hunter & Hare VINTAGE

28 🛍 MAP P42, H5

A lovely store specializing in well-curated consignment clothing and accessories for women, this is the place to head to if you've left your summer frock at home by mistake. Smiley staff can point you in the right direction and prices are enticingly reasonable. It's not all used togs; there's also jewelry, greeting cards and beauty products from local artisan producers. (☎604-559-4273; www.hunterandhare.com; 334 W Pender St, Downtown; ⌚11am-7pm Mon-Sat, noon-5pm Sun; 🚌14)

Little Sister's Book & Art Emporium BOOKS

29 🛍 MAP P42, D5

Launched almost 40 years ago as one of the only LGBTIQ+ bookshops in Canada, Little Sister's is a bazaar of queer-positive tomes, plus magazines, clothing and toys of the adult type. If this is your first visit to Vancouver, it's a great place to network with the local 'gayborhood.' Check the noticeboards for events and announcements from the community. (☎604-669-1753; www.littlesisters.ca; 1238 Davie St, West End; ⌚9am-10pm Sun-Thu, to 11am Fri & Sat; 🚌6)

Mink Chocolates FOOD

30 🛍 MAP P42, G4

If chocolate is the main food group in your book, follow your candy-primed nose to this choccy shop and cafe in the downtown core. Select from the kaleidoscopic array of colorfully boxed ganache-filled bars, including top-seller Mermaid's Choice, then hit the drinks bar for the best velvety hot choc you've ever tasted. Then have another. (☎604-633-2451; www.minkchocolates.com; 863 W Hastings St, Downtown; ⌚7:30am-6pm Mon-Fri, 9:30am-5pm Sat & Sun; 📶; S Waterfront)

Walking Tour 🥾

Lower Lonsdale Wander

This easy loop will take you into the heart of North Vancouver's reinvented shipyards area. You'll discover a once-gritty industrial swathe that's been reinvigorated with oceanfront attractions, scenic boardwalk promenades and a full menu of tasty pit stops. Take your time here; there's lots to discover.

Walk Facts

Start Lonsdale Quay SeaBus Station

End Burgoo

Length 1km; one hour

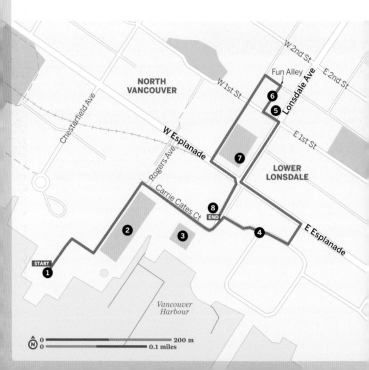

❶ Lonsdale Quay

After your 15-minute SeaBus voyage from Vancouver's Waterfront Station, walk up the ramp at North Van's Lonsdale Quay and turn right.

❷ Lonsdale Quay Market

The **Lonsdale Quay Market** (☎604-985-6261; www.lonsdalequay. com; 123 Carrie Cates Ct, North Vancouver; ◷9am-7pm; 📶; ⛴Lonsdale Quay SeaBus) is lined with food stands and artisan stores; there's even an on-site microbrewery if you're thirsty.

❸ Polygon Gallery

A symbol of the area's revitalization, visit the striking **Polygon Gallery** (☎604-986-1351; www.the polygon.ca; 101 Carrie Cates Ct, North Vancouver; by donation; ◷10am-5pm Tue-Sun; ⛴Lonsdale Quay SeaBus). And check out the upper-floor views across to downtown Vancouver.

❹ Old Wallace Shipyards

Look for the large-format photo of the yesteryear shipyard, showing hundreds of tough-as-nails men gearing up for work.

❺ Lift Breakfast Bakery

Revive yourself with coffee and treats at **Lift Breakfast Bakery** (☎778-388-5438; www.lift onlonsdale.ca; 101 Lonsdale Ave, North Vancouver; mains $14-26; ◷7am-4pm Mon, Wed & Thu, to 10pm Fri & Sat, 9am-10pm Sun; 📶; 🚌239).

❻ Fun Alley

Right next door, a tiny back alley has been painted like a walk-through kaleidoscope. It's camera time.

❼ Mo's General Store

Quirky souvenir shopping is easy at **Mo's General Store** (☎604-928-7827; www.mosgeneralstore.com; 51 Lonsdale Ave, North Vancouver; ◷8am-6pm Mon, to 8pm Tue-Sat, 9am-6pm Sun; ⛴Lonsdale Quay SeaBus). Where else will you find woolen avocado socks?

❽ Burgoo

End your day out with dinner at this popular bistro-style **restaurant** (☎604-904-0933; www.burgoo.ca; 3 Lonsdale Ave, North Vancouver; mains $14-18; ◷11am-10pm; ⛴Lonsdale Quay SeaBus). The SeaBus terminal, and a short hop back to downtown Vancouver, are just steps away.

Worth a Trip 🔭
Brave the Leg-Wobbling Capilano Suspension Bridge Park

One of Metro Vancouver's most-visited attractions is jam-packed with tour buses in summer. But there's a reason everyone's coming: that jelly-leg-triggering suspension bridge over the roiling, tree-flanked waters of Capilano Canyon is one of the region's most memorable highlights. Also, a host of extra attractions has been added to this scenery-hugging park over the years.

www.capbridge.com

3735 Capilano Rd, North Vancouver

adult/child $47/15

🕗 8am-8pm May-Aug, reduced hours off-season

🚉 Free shuttle from downtown or transit bus 236 from Lonsdale Quay

Bridge

Starting life as a simple rope-and-plank span in 1880, the bridge's current steel cable iteration stretches 137m: wide enough to fly two Boeing 747s wing-to-wing underneath (strangely, no one has tried this yet). Swaying gently as you walk across (unless a group of deliberately heavy-footed teenagers is stomping nearby), most first-timers steady themselves on the cable 'handrail' but usually let go as they progress and adapt to the leg-wobbling sensation. Don't forget to stop midway for photos of the mountain-framed, tree-lined vista.

Park

The bridge is the star attraction but there's much more to keep you occupied here. Check the outdoor historic displays and First Nations totem poles before you head across. And once you're on the other side, explore the short trails and wooden walkways that take you deeper into the surrounding forest. Look out for **Big Doug**, a 350-year-old Douglas fir tree that stretches 60 meters into the sky. Also peruse the kid-friendly displays on the area's flora and fauna, from woodpeckers to banana slugs.

Cliffwalk

Head back over to the other side of the bridge (you probably won't need to hold on so tightly this time), turn left and look for the entrance to Cliffwalk (pictured), another included-with-admission extra. Descend the steps here and you'll soon find yourself on a lofty steel bridge walkway that clings tenaciously to the rockside, offering great views of the watery canyon below (especially at several scenic stop-off points). The scariest part? The glass-bottomed sections that make your legs tingle in protest.

★ Top Tips

o Arrive soon after opening time to avoid the relentless summer crush.

o Take the free year-round shuttle bus from downtown Vancouver to the park's entrance.

o The gift shop is one of Metro Vancouver's biggest; you can tick off your entire souvenir list in one go here.

o Grouse Mountain is 10 minutes north on the same 236 transit bus route.

✕ Take a Break

The park's bistro-like **Cliff House Restaurant** (mains $22-26; ⏱11am-5pm; 📶) serves great fish and chips plus local craft beer; peruse the yesteryear Capilano photos on the walls.

Explore ◈

Gastown & Chinatown

The old-town district where Vancouver began, Gastown has been transformed, its heritage buildings now housing top-rated boutiques and restaurants. Almost as old, historic Chinatown is one of Canada's largest and has started gentrifying even faster – hence the new condo blocks that make the ancient grocery stores look slightly shabby. Explore both of these fascinating adjoining areas on foot.

The Short List

○ **Alibi Room (p72)** *Tucking into the city's best array of regional craft beers while rubbing shoulders with the locals at one of the long, candlelit tables; small sampler glasses recommended.*

○ **Eastside Flea (p74)** *Nosing around the artisan stalls, vintage-clothing stands and tasty food trucks at this regular hipster market.*

○ **St Lawrence Restaurant (p70)** *Feasting on fine French-Canadian cuisine and feeling like you're hanging out in old-town Montréal.*

Getting There & Around

🚇 SkyTrain's Waterfront Station is at the western edge of Gastown. Stadium-Chinatown Station is on the edge of Chinatown, due south of Gastown.

🚌 Bus 14 heads northwards from downtown's Granville St then along Hastings, handy for both Gastown and Chinatown. Buses 3, 4, 7 and 8 also service the area.

🚗 There is metered parking throughout Gastown and Chinatown.

Gastown & Chinatown Map on p66

Dominion Building SVETLANASF / GETTY IMAGES ©

Top Experience 📷

Get Your True Crime Fix at the Vancouver Police Museum

◎ MAP P66, E3

The city's best hidden-gem museum, located in a heritage brick building that formerly housed the local coroner's court and autopsy room, does a great job of poking at the seedy underbelly of Vancouver's not-too-distant past. Head upstairs here and check your nervous disposition at the entrance.

📞 604-665-3346

www.vancouverpolice
museum.ca

240 E Cordova St

adult/child $12/8

🕑 9am-5pm Tue-Sat

🚊 3

Morgue & More

The museum's first room is the restored coroner's court. Its formerly obscured windows and elaborately beamed ceiling have now been uncovered for viewing, while the exhibits explore the history of Vancouver's police force. As you move through the rooms, the displays take on a darker hue until you find yourself in the autopsy room. Decommissioned in 1980 but almost unchanged since (which is why it's often used for film productions), the stainless steel dissection tables (pictured) are a stark reminder of this room's grisly-but-essential purpose. Peruse the human tissue samples (some with bullet holes) on the walls.

Crime Cases

Just before the spine-chilling autopsy room, look out for a row of display cases filled with photos, exhibits and a skull or two. Each cabinet illuminates a notorious real-life crime from Vancouver's past. No punches are pulled – some crime scene photos depict huge pools of blood – but it's well worth stopping to encounter some hair-raising yesteryear tales some Vancouverites can still recall first-hand.

Sins of the City

If you really want to get to know Vancouver's crime-soaked past, book an evocative Sins of the City (p67) walking tour. Taking to the historic streets around the neighborhood, these themed tours illuminate the area's darkly illicit heritage, from brothels to opium dens. The tours last up to two hours and run regularly from April to October.

★ **Top Tips**

o If you're here sometime between September and April, catch a monthly movie screening in the morgue – if you dare.

o Check ahead for fascinating speaker talks, covering a wide array of crime-related themes.

o There's a bookcase of for-sale crime tomes near the front desk, often including local-focused titles *Cold Case Vancouver* and *The Last Gang in Town*.

✕ **Take a Break**

Nip into the nearby Ovaltine Cafe (p68), an old-school diner reminder of gritty yesteryear Vancouver.

And if you need a stiff drink after all that blood and gore, hit the Alibi Room (p72), complete with one of Vancouver's best craft-beer selections.

Top Experience 📷

Bask in the Calm of Dr Sun Yat-Sen Classical Chinese Garden

Reputedly the first Chinese 'scholars' garden' ever built outside China and opened just in time for Vancouver's Expo '86 world exposition, this oasis of tranquility is one of the city's most-beloved ornamental green spaces. Framed by tile-topped walls and centered on a mirror-calm pond fringed by twisting trees, its covered walkways are a calming respite from clamorous Chinatown.

◎ MAP P66, D4

www.vancouverchinese
garden.com

578 Carrall St, Chinatown

adult/child $14/10

🕙 9:30am-7pm mid-
Jun– Aug, 10am-6pm Sep &
May–mid-Jun, 10am-4:30pm
Oct-Apr

S Stadium-Chinatown

Harmonious Design

With symbol-heavy architecture that feels centuries old – walled courtyards, small bridges, flare-roof buildings and sidewalks fashioned from mosaics of patterned pebbles – this highly photogenic garden is also studded with large, eerie **limestone rocks** that look like they were imported from the moon. In reality, they were hauled all the way from Lake Tai in China. They give the garden a mystical, almost otherworldly feel.

Natural Jewels

The garden's large, lily-pad-covered **pond** is often as calm as a sheet of green glass – except when its resident neon-orange koi carp break the surface in hopes of snagging food from passersby (don't feed them, though). They're not the only critters that call this watery haven home. Look carefully at some of the rocks poking from the water and you'll spot dozing turtles basking in the sun. Ducks, frogs and beady-eyed herons are also frequently spotted. Plantwise, you'll find pine, bamboo, flowering plum trees and pots of decades-old bonsai trees that look like the diminutive offspring of Ents.

Freebie Alternative

Located right next door to the paid-entry garden, there's a fancy-free gratis alternative that shares some of its sibling's classical features. The **Dr Sun Yat-Sen Park** was inspired by the adjoining attraction and shares the same pond. It also has nature-fringed walkways encircled by tile-topped walls and its main feature is a small, red-roofed, Chinese-style pavilion that makes for great photos, especially when you catch it reflected off the pond.

★ Top Tips

o Arrive early on summer days to experience the garden's tranquility before the crowds roll in.

o Tours run hourly during the summer peak, but also several times a day throughout the rest of the year. Check the website schedule and time your visit accordingly.

o Peruse the gift shop before you leave; it's well stocked with tea and traditional calligraphy tools.

o The towering Chinatown Millennium Gate is one block away if you still have some battery power left in your camera.

✕ Take a Break

Mix up your cultures with a German-style currywurst lunch, a few minutes walk away at Bestie (p68) on E Pender St.

For dinner, E Pender is also home to Sai Woo (p70), the perfect place for cocktails and soy-ginger chicken.

Walking Tour 🚶

Chinatown Culture & History Crawl

One of North America's largest and most historic Chinatown districts is perfect for on-foot exploring. Keep your eyes peeled for tile-topped heritage buildings, traditional grocery and apothecary stores and street lamps adorned with fierce-looking golden dragons.

Walk Facts

Start Chinatown Millennium Gate

End Vancouver Police Museum

Length 1.5km; one hour

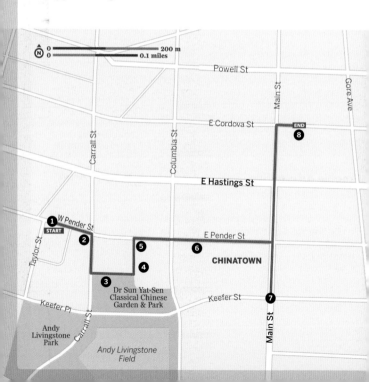

❶ Chinatown Millennium Gate

The grand entrance to Chinatown was only erected in 2000 but it's a fitting testament to the neighborhood's longevity. Crane your neck for the colorful upper-level decoration and don't miss the ground-level lion statues.

❷ Jack Chow Building

Once in the *Guinness Book of Records* as the world's narrowest commercial building, this slender office (p67) is a magnet for visitors keen to find curious local sites.

❸ Dr Sun Yat-Sen Classical Chinese Garden

A peaceful respite from Chinatown's clamorous streets, wander the pebble-cobbled pathways of this popular horticultural site (p62), watching for carp and turtles in the mirror-calm pond en route.

❹ Bronze Memorial

Near the garden's entrance, wander across the small paved plaza and look for an intriguing bronze memorial set in bright red wall tiles. It recalls the contribution of Chinese works to building Canada's vast railway system.

❺ The 'Other' Chinatown Gate

A few steps away is a ghostly white alternative Chinatown gate. This one is smaller and was built for Vancouver's Expo '86 and moved here after the big event.

❻ Sai Woo's Menu

If you've yet to make dinner plans, peruse your options at this popular restaurant (p70). And make sure you snap a photo of its neon rooster sign, a replica of an original that was here for decades.

❼ Keefer St Stores

Chinatown is lined with a fascinating fusion of old-fashioned and far newer storefronts. Exploring Keefer, you'll find traditional grocery shops next to hipster coffeehouses.

❽ Vancouver Police Museum

The city's crime-addled past is on colorful display at this under-the-radar museum (p60). Don't miss its historic crime exhibits and preserved mortuary room.

Gastown & Chinatown

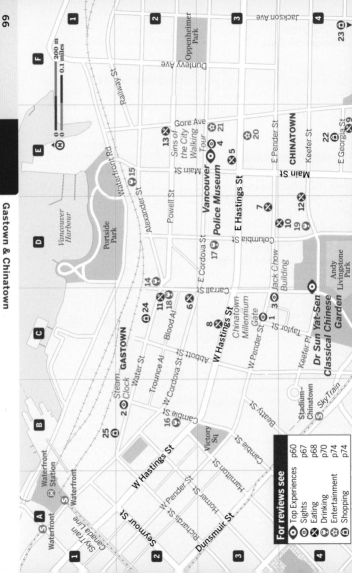

Steam Clock
GASTOWN
Waterfront Station
SkyTrain Canada Line
Waterfront

Vancouver Harbour

Portside Park

Sins of the City Walking Tour

Oppenheimer Park

Gore Ave

Railway St

Dunlevy Ave

Waterfront Rd

Alexander St

Powell St

E Cordova St

W Hastings St

E Hastings St

Main St

CHINATOWN

E Pender St

Keefer St

E Georgia St

Jackson Ave

Vancouver Police Museum

Chinatown Millennium Gate

Jack Chow Building

Dr Sun Yat-Sen Classical Chinese Garden

Andy Livingstone Park

Stadium–Chinatown
SkyTrain

Victory Sq

W Hastings St

W Pender St

Dunsmuir St

Seymour St

Richards St

Homer St

Hamilton St

Cambie St

Beatty St

Taylor St

Keefer Pl

Columbia St

Carrall St

Abbott St

Cambie St

Water St

Trounce Al

Blood Al

W Cordova St

200 m
0.1 miles

For reviews see	
○ Top Experiences	p60
○ Sights	p67
○ Eating	p68
○ Drinking	p70
○ Entertainment	p74
○ Shopping	p74

Sights

Chinatown Millennium Gate
LANDMARK

1 MAP P66, C3

Inaugurated in 2002, Chinatown's towering entrance is the landmark most visitors look for. Stand well back, since the decoration is mostly on its lofty upper reaches, an elaborately painted section topped with a terracotta-tiled roof. The characters inscribed on its eastern front implore you to 'Remember the past and look forward to the future.' (cnr W Pender & Taylor Sts, Chinatown; **S** Stadium-Chinatown)

Steam Clock
LANDMARK

2 MAP P66, B2

Halfway along Water St, this tourist magnet lures the cameras with its tooting steam whistle. Built in 1977, the clock's mechanism is driven by electricity; only the pipes on top are steam fueled. It sounds every 15 minutes, and marks each hour with little whistling symphonies. (cnr Water & Cambie Sts, Gastown; **S** Waterfront)

Jack Chow Building
NOTABLE BUILDING

3 MAP P66, C3

This unusual spot was known for decades as the Sam Kee Building until Jack Chow Insurance changed the name and spruced it up. Listed in the *Guinness Book of World Records* as the planet's shallowest commercial building, it includes a

---

Toppling of the Gassy Jack Statue

John Deighton, known as 'Gassy Jack', is seen by many as Vancouver's founder. The late-19th-century bar owner and businessman, who gave Gastown its name, has become an increasingly controversial figure in recent years, due to his marriage to a 12-year-old Indigenous girl in 1870, and his statue, which stood in Maple Tree Square, was toppled by protesters in 2022 during an annual march for Missing & Murdered Indigenous Women and Girls.

---

synchronized musical light show on the outside of the structure. (www.jackchow.com; 8 W Pender St, Chinatown; **S** Stadium-Chinatown)

Sins of the City Walking Tour
WALKING

4 MAP P66, E3

If your criminal interests are triggered by the Vancouver Police Museum (p60), take one of its excellent Sins of the City walking tours, which weave through Gastown and Chinatown in search of former brothels, opium dens, gambling houses and more. Lasting up to two hours, the tours are a great way to see the less-salubrious side of the metropolis. (☑604-665-3346; www.sinsofthecity.ca; 240 E Cordova St, Vancouver Police Museum; adult/student $18/14; ⏰ Apr-Oct; ☑14)

Beyond the Steam Clock

Walking along Water St, you'll likely bump into a gaggle of visitors snapping photos of the **Steam Clock** (p67), a free-standing timepiece famous for its time-marking steam-whistle displays. But Gastown is full of additional photo opportunities, so long as you know where to go. Start in Maple Tree Sq; look for cool architectural details at the **Dominion Building** and the **Flack Block**; and try to get the perfect angle to snap the old and new neon 'W' signs at the renovated **Woodward's Building**.

Eating

Ovaltine Cafe   DINER $

5 MAP P66, E3

Like being inside Edward Hopper's *Nighthawks* diner painting, this time-capsule greasy spoon instantly transports you to the 1940s. Snag a booth alongside the hospital-green walls or, better yet, slide onto a tape-repaired spinning stool at the long counter. Truck-stop coffee is *de rigueur* here, alongside burgers, sandwiches and fried breakfasts that haven't changed in decades (yes, that's liver and onions on the menu). (604-685-7021; www.facebook.com/ovaltinecafe; 251 E Hastings St, Chinatown; mains $7-10; 6:30am-3pm Mon-Sat, 6:30am-2pm Sun; 14)

Tacofino Taco Bar   MEXICAN $

6 MAP P66, C2

Food-truck favorite Tacofino made an instant splash with this huge, handsome dining room with stylish geometric-patterned floors, hive-like lampshades and a tiny back patio. The simple menu focuses on a handful of taco options plus nachos, soups and a selection of beer, agave and tequila flights. Fish tacos are the top seller, but we love the supertender lamb *birria* version. (604-899-7907; www.tacofino. com; 15 W Cordova St, Gastown; tacos from $6; 11:30am-10pm Sun-Wed, 11:30am-midnight Thu-Sat; 14)

Bestie   GERMAN $

7 MAP P66, D3

Like a food truck with a permanent home, this white-walled hole-in-the-wall specializes in Berlin-style currywursts – hearty sausages slathered in curry sauce, served with crunchy fries. It's popular with passing hipsters, so arrive off-peak for a chance to snag the little cubby-hole window table: the best in the house. Fresh-baked pretzels and a well-curated array of local craft beers add to the mix. (604-620-1175; www.facebook.com/bestie wurst; 105 E Pender St, Chinatown; mains $4-11; 11:30am-10pm Sun-Thu, 11:30am-midnight Fri & Sat; 3)

Save on Meats

DINER $

8 🌶 MAP P66, C3

A former old-school butcher shop that's been transformed into a popular hipster diner. Slide into a booth or hop on a swivel chair at the superlong counter and tuck into comfort dishes. They range from a good-value $6 all-day breakfast to the satisfying SOM burger, paired with a heaping tangle of 'haystack' fries. Add a BC-brewed Persephone beer to keep things lively. (☎604-569-3568; www.saveonmeats.ca; 43 W Hastings St, Gastown; mains $6-15; ⊙11am-7pm Sun-Thu, 11am-11pm Fri & Sat; 🛜🍴; 🚌14)

Phnom Penh

VIETNAMESE, CAMBODIAN $$

9 🌶 MAP P66, E4

The dishes at this bustling, local-legend joint are split between Cambodian and Vietnamese soul-food classics. It's the highly addictive chicken wings and their lovely pepper sauce that keep regulars loyal. Once you've piled up the bones, dive back in for round two: papaya salad, butter beef and spring rolls show just how good a street-food-inspired Asian menu can be. (☎604-682-5777; www.phnompenhrestaurant.ca; 244 E Georgia St, Chinatown; mains $8-18; ⊙10am-9pm Mon-Thu, 10am-10pm Fri-Sun; 🚌3)

Bestie

ALEXANDRE MOYEN / LONELY PLANET ©

Sai Woo

ASIAN $$

10 🍴 MAP P66, D4

There's a film-set look to the exterior of this contemporary restaurant that resembles a replica of an old Hong Kong restaurant. But the long, slender interior is a candlelit cave with a lounge-like vibe. Expect a wide array of Asian dishes, from Szechuan spicy-beef noodles to Korean-style barbecued-pork pancakes, and consider the happy hour (5pm to 6pm) with half-price dumplings. (604-568-1117; www.saiwoo.ca; 158 E Pender, Chinatown; mains $13-23; 5pm-midnight Tue-Sat, 5-9pm Sun; 3)

MeeT in Gastown

VEGAN $$

11 🍴 MAP P66, C2

Serving great vegan comfort dishes without the rabbit-food approach, this wildly popular spot can be clamorously busy at times. But it's worth the wait for a wide-ranging array of herbivore- and carnivore-pleasing dishes, from rice bowls and mac 'n' cheese (made from vegan cashew 'cheese') to hearty burgers and poutine-like fries slathered in nut-based miso gravy (our recommendation). (604-696-1111; www.meetonmain.com; 12 Water St, Gastown; mains $10-16; 11am-11pm Sun-Thu, 11am-midnight Fri & Sat; ; M Waterfront)

Bao Bei

CHINESE $$

12 🍴 MAP P66, D4

Reinterpreting a Chinatown heritage building with hipteresque flourishes, this Chinese brasserie is a seductive dinner destination. Bringing a contemporary edge to Asian cuisine are tapas-sized, MSG-free dishes such as *shao bing* (stuffed Chinese flatbread), delectable dumplings and spicy-chicken steamed buns. There's also an enticing drinks menu guaranteed to make you linger, especially if you dive into the inventive cocktails. (604-688-0876; www.bao-bei.ca; 163 Keefer St, Chinatown; small plates $6-23; 5:30pm-midnight Mon-Sat, 5:30-11pm Sun; 3)

St Lawrence Restaurant

FRENCH $$$

13 🍴 MAP P66, E2

Resembling a handsome wood-floored bistro that's been teleported straight from Montréal, this sparkling, country-chic dining room is a Railtown superstar. The Québecois approach carries over onto a small menu of elevated, perfectly prepared old-school mains such as trout in brown-butter sauce and the utterly delicious duck-leg confit with sausage. French-Canadian special-occasion dining at its finest. (604-620-3800; www.stlawrencerestaurant.com; 269 Powell St; mains $34-44; 5:30-10:30pm Tue-Sun; 4)

Drinking

Guilt & Co

BAR

14 🍺 MAP P66, D2

This cavelike subterranean bar, beneath Gastown's brick-cobbled

Vancouver's Oldest Street?

Just a few weeks after renaming itself Vancouver in 1886 (no one liked the original name 'Granville,' nor the insalubrious slang name 'Gastown' that preceded it), the fledgling city of around 1000 homes burnt almost to the ground in what came to be known as the **Great Fire**. But the locals weren't about to jump on the next boat out of town. Within days, plans were drawn up for a new city, this time favoring brick and stone over wood.

Starting Again

The first buildings to be erected radiated from Maple Tree Sq, in particular along Carrall St. This short thoroughfare still exists today, linking the historic center of Gastown to Chinatown. Take a stroll along Carrall and you'll spot some grand buildings from Vancouver's early days. Some of the sturdiest structures around, they'll likely survive for many years, whether or not there's another fire.

Saving Gastown

If you'd visited 30 years ago, however, you would have seen many of these buildings seemingly on their last legs. This part of Vancouver hadn't attracted development or investment for years and Carrall St's old taverns, hotels and storefronts were spiraling into skid-row degradation. Two things changed the inevitable: firstly, historians and heritage fans banded together to draw attention to the area's role in the city's founding years, a campaign that culminated in a national historic site designation in 2010. Secondly, gentrification took hold.

Upside of Gentrification?

With few areas around the city still left to 'enhance,' the developers finally came back to Gastown. While gentrification has many vocal detractors, an undeniable positive is that it has preserved and protected this neighborhood's historic buildings for decades to come. Carrall St's brick-and-stone landmarks have, for the most part, been sympathetically restored and renovated, giving many of them a new lease on life.

sidewalks, is also a brilliant venue to catch a tasty side dish of live music. Most shows are pay-what-you-can and can range from trumpet jazz to heartfelt singer-songwriters. Drinks-wise, there's a great cocktail list plus a small array of draft beers (and many more in cans and bottles). Avoid weekends when there are often queues. (www.guiltandcompany.com; 1 Alexander St, Gastown; ⊘7pm-late; ⓢWaterfront)

Vancouver's Best Art Fest

During November's **Eastside Culture Crawl** (www.culturecrawl.ca; ☻mid-Nov), hundreds of local artists open their studios, houses and workshops to art-loving visitors who wander from site to site. Festival locations stretch eastwards from the north end of Main St and visitors spend their time walking the streets looking for the next hot spot, which is typically just around the corner. Look out for the occasional street performer keeping things lively and be sure to incorporate a coffee-shop pit stop along the way. The event is a great opportunity to buy one-of-a-kind artwork souvenirs for that difficult person back home (you know the one).

Alibi Room   PUB

15 🖼 MAP P66, E2

Vancouver's best craft-beer tavern pours a near-legendary roster of 50-plus drafts, many from celebrated BC breweries including Four Winds, Yellow Dog and Dageraad. Hipsters and veteran-ale fans alike love the 'frat bat': choose your own four samples or ask to be surprised. Check the board for new guest casks and stick around for a gastropub dinner at one of the chatty long tables. (📞604-623-3383; www.alibi.ca; 157 Alexander St, Gastown; ☻5-11:30pm Mon-Thu, 5pm-12:30am Fri, 10am-12:30am Sat, 10am-11:30pm Sun; 🛜; 🚌4)

Revolver   COFFEE

16 🖼 MAP P66, B2

Gastown's coolest see-and-be-seen coffee shop, Revolver has never lost its hipster crown. But it's remained at the top of the Vancouver coffee-mug tree via a serious commitment to serving expertly prepared top-quality java. Aim for a little booth table or, if they're taken (they usually are), hit the large communal table room next door. (📞604-558-4444; www.revolvercoffee.ca; 325 Cambie St, Gastown; ☻7:30am-6pm Mon-Fri, 9am-6pm Sat; 🛜; 🚌14)

Back and Forth Bar   BAR

17 🖼 MAP P66, D3

There's an inviting, den-like feel to this cool-but-friendly games-room bar, where six ping-pong tables combine perfectly with a 12-tap beer selection (local microbrews and 'ironic' Lucky Lager included). An ideal late-night hangout, book ahead for a table (from $10 to $25 per hour, with lowest rates from Sunday to Tuesday) or just indulge in some giggle-triggering Jenga and Pictionary. (📞604-564-7664; www.backandforthbar.com; 303 Columbia St, Chinatown; ☻4pm-2am Sun-Thu, 4pm-3am Fri & Sat; 🛜; 🚌14)

Six Acres

BAR

18   MAP P66, C2

Gastown's coziest tavern, you can cover all the necessary food groups via the carefully chosen draft- and bottled-beer list here. There's a small, animated summer patio situated out the front but inside (especially upstairs) is great for hiding in a chatty, candlelit corner and working your way through the craft brews – plus a shared small plate or three (we like the sausage board). (📞604-488-0110; www.sixacres.ca; 203 Carrall St, Gastown; ⏱11:30am-11:30pm Sun-Thu, 11:30am-12:30am Fri & Sat; 📶; 📦4)

Keefer Bar

COCKTAIL BAR

19   MAP P66, D4

This dark, narrow and atmospheric bar in Chinatown has been claimed by local cocktail-loving coolsters since day one. Drop in for a full evening of liquid taste-tripping and you'll have a blast. From perfectly prepared rosemary gimlets and tart blood moons to an excellent whiskey menu and some tasty tapas (we like the steam buns), it offers up a great night out. (📞604-688-1961; www.thekeeferbar.com; 135 Keefer St, Chinatown; ⏱5pm-1am Sun-Thu, 5pm-2am Fri & Sat; Ⓢ Stadium-Chinatown)

Revolver

Entertainment

Rickshaw Theatre LIVE MUSIC

20 ⭐ MAP P66, E3

Revamped from its grungy 1970s incarnation, the funky Rickshaw shows that Eastside gentrification can be positive. The stage of choice for many punk and indie acts, it's an excellent place to see a band. There's a huge mosh area near the stage and rows of theater-style seats at the back. (📞604-681-8915; www.liveatrickshaw.com; 254 E Hastings St, Chinatown; tickets from $15; 🚌14)

Firehall Arts Centre THEATER

21 ⭐ MAP P66, E3

One of the leading players in Vancouver's independent-theater scene, this intimate, studio-sized venue is located inside a historic former fire station. It presents culturally diverse contemporary drama and dance, with an emphasis on emerging talent. A key venue during July's annual Dancing on the Edge festival (www.dancingontheedge.org), it also has a convivial licensed lounge on-site. (📞604-689-0926; www.firehallartscentre.ca; 280 E Cordova St, Chinatown; tickets from $30; 🚌14)

Shopping

Massy Books BOOKS

22 🔒 MAP P66, E4

A former pop-up favorite with a now-permanent Chinatown location, this delightful bookstore is lined with tall stacks of well-curated, mostly used titles. There's an impressively large selection of Aboriginal-themed books, alongside good selections covering travel, history and literature – plus a bargain $1 cart outside. Love mysteries? Try finding the store's secret room, hidden behind a pushable bookcase door. (📞604-721-4405; www.massybooks.com; 229 E Georgia St, Chinatown; ⏰10am-6pm Sun-Wed, 10am-8pm Thu-Sat; 🚌3)

Eastside Flea MARKET

23 🔒 MAP P66, F4

A size upgrade from its previous venue has delivered a cavernous market hall of hip arts and crafts-isans hawking everything

Massy Books

JOHN LEE / LONELY PLANET ©

from handmade chocolate bars to intricate jewelry and a humungous array of cool-ass vintage clothing. Give yourself plenty of time to hang out here; there's a pool table and retro arcade machines plus food trucks and a long bar serving local craft beer. (www.eastsideflea.com; 550 Malkin Ave, Eastside Studios; $3-5; ☺11am-5pm Sat & Sun, once or twice a month; ▣22)

John Fluevog Shoes   SHOES

24 🔒 MAP P66, C2

Like an art gallery for shoes, this alluringly cavernous store showcases the famed footwear of local designer Fluevog, whose men's and women's boots and brogues are what Doc Martens would have become if they'd stayed interesting and cutting edge. Pick up that pair of thigh-hugging dominatrix boots you've always wanted or settle on some designer loafers that would make anyone walk tall. (☎604-688-6228; www.fluevog.com; 65 Water St, Gastown; ☺10am-7pm Mon-Wed & Sat, to 8pm Thu & Fri, noon-6pm Sun; Ⓢ Waterfront)

Vintage Shopping

Gastown and Chinatown are studded with cool stores but a growing number of vintage shops have also popped up on area side streets; check out several on Columbia St between Pender and Hastings.

Herschel Supply Co   FASHION & ACCESSORIES

25 🔒 MAP P66, B1

The friendly flagship store of this hot, Vancouver-based bags-and-accessories brand is a must-see for Herschel fans. Inside a beautifully restored, artwork-lined Gastown heritage building (check out the waterfront views from the back windows), you'll find a huge array of the company's signature daypacks, plus wallets, totes, pouches and clothing lines. Give yourself plenty of perusing time; you're gonna need it. (☎604-620-1155; www.herschel.com; 347 Water St, Gastown; ☺10am-7pm Mon-Wed & Sat, 10am-9pm Thu & Fri, 11am-6pm Sun; Ⓢ Waterfront)

Explore ⬡
Yaletown & Granville Island

Straddling tranquil False Creek, these opposite shore-line neighborhoods exemplify Vancouver's development in recent decades. A former rail-yard district on the edge of downtown, Yaletown is now lined with posh restaurants and boutiques. Across the water, Granville Island was an industrial hub before being transformed in the 1970s into a haven of theaters, artisan studios and Western Canada's best public market.

The Short List

○ **Granville Island Public Market (p78)** *Gathering some treats before catching a busker or two outside.*

○ **Vancouver Whitecaps (p91)** *Joining the crowds for a BC Place pro-soccer game; face-painting optional.*

Getting There & Around

🚌 Number 50 from downtown stops near Granville Island's entrance. Bus 10 stops on the south side of Granville Bridge, a five-minute stroll from the island.

🚊 The Canada Line from downtown stops at Yaletown-Roundhouse Station.

🚗 Yaletown has metered parking. Granville Island has free and paid parking.

Miniferries Granville Island is accessible by miniferry from False Creek's north shore.

Yaletown & Granville Island Map on p84

Granville Bridge (p81) RIC JAGYNO / SHUTTERSTOCK ©

Top Experience 📷
Snack Your Way Around the Granville Island Public Market

A foodie extravaganza specializing in deli treats and pyramids of shiny fruit and vegetables, this is one of North America's finest public markets. It's ideal for whiling away an afternoon, snacking on goodies in the sun among the buskers outside or sheltering from the rain with a market tour. You'll also find side dishes of (admittedly inedible) arts and crafts.

◎ MAP P84, G4

📞 604-666-6655

www.granvilleisland.com/public-market

Johnston St, Granville Island

🕘 9am-7pm

🚌 50, ⛴ miniferries

Taste-tripping

Come hungry: there are dozens of food stands to weave your way around at the market. Among the must-see vendors are **Oyama Sausage Company**, replete with hundreds of smoked sausages and cured meats; **Benton Brothers Fine Cheese**, with its full complement of amazing curdy goodies from British Columbia (BC) and around the world (look for anything by Farm House Natural Cheese from Agassiz, BC); and **Granville Island Tea Company** (Hawaiian rooibos recommended), with its tasting bar and more than 150 steep-tastic varieties to choose from. Baked goodies also abound: abandon your diet at **Lee's Donuts** and **Siegel's Bagels**, where the naughty cheese-stuffed baked varieties are not to be missed. And don't worry: there's always room for a wafer-thin album-sized 'cinnamon record' from **Stuart's Baked Goods**. French-themed **L'Epicerie Rotisserie and Gourmet Shop** has been a popular addition to the market. It sells vinegars, olive oils and delicious house-cooked dishes to go.

In the unlikely event you're still hungry, there's also a small international food court: avoid off-peak dining if you want to snag a table and indulge in a good-value selection that runs from Mexican tacos to German sausages. And if you want to dive into some regional seasonal produce, there's even a **farmers market** just outside the market building between June and October where you can even sample BC-made booze.

Arts & Crafts

Once you've eaten your fill, take a look at some of the market's other stands. There's a cool arts and crafts focus here, especially among the collection of day vendors that dot the market and change every week. Hand-knitted hats, hand-painted ceramics, framed art photography and

★ Top Tips

○ Arrive early to sidestep the summer crowds, which peak in the afternoons.

○ If you're driving, weekdays are the easiest times to find on-island parking.

○ The food court is the island's best-value dining. But tables are scarce at peak times.

○ Birdwatcher? Look for the cormorants nesting under the Granville Bridge span.

✕ Take a Break

Just across from the Public Market, A Bread Affair (p88) serves excellent house-baked treats plus good-value gourmet sandwiches.

Fancy-free local favorite Tony's Fish & Oyster Cafe (p88) serves the island's best fish and chips; dine off-peak since table spots are limited.

quirky carvings will make for excellent one-of-a-kind souvenirs. Further artisan stands are added to the roster in the run-up to Christmas, if you happen to be here at that time. For more information on the sorts of day vendors that appear at the market, visit www.gidva.org.

Insider's Tour

If you're a hungry culinary fan, the delicious guided market walk organized by **Vancouver Foodie Tours** (📞604-295-8844; www.foodietours.ca; tours from $65) is the way to go. This leisurely stomach-stuffer (adult/child $70/60) weaves around the vendors and includes several tasting stops that will quickly fill you up. It also caters to vegetarians if you mention it when you book. The company runs friendly tasting tours in

other parts of the city, too, if you're keen to keep eating.

Forgotten Past

The Public Market is the centerpiece of one of Canada's most impressive urban regeneration projects – and the main reason it has been so successful. Built as a district for small factories in the early part of the last century, Granville Island – which has also been called Mud Island and Industrial Island over the years – had declined into a paint-peeled no-go area by the 1960s. But the abandoned sheds began attracting artists and theater groups by the 1970s, and the old buildings slowly started springing back to life with some much-needed repairs and upgrades. Within a few years, new theaters, restaurants and studios

Granville Island's Industrial Side

Many visitors spend their time on Granville Island at the Public Market end, nipping between the myriad shops and studios. But heading a few minutes along Johnston St offers some reminders of the time when this human-made peninsula (since it's joined to the mainland, it's not actually an island) was home to dozens of hard-toiling factories making everything from chains to iron hinges.

One million cubic yards of landfill was tipped into False Creek to create the island in the early 20th century, but almost all the reminders of its gritty first few years have been lost. Almost. The area's oldest tenant, **Ocean Concrete,** is a cement maker that began here in 1917 and now cranks out enough product to build a 10-story tower block every week. It also does a great job of being a good neighbor. A Vancouver Biennale initiative saw the company's six gigantic waterfront silos transformed into huge multicolored figures, while its annual April **open house** event is hotly anticipated by local families.

Continue along Johnston a little further and you'll come to a second monument to the past: a landmark **yellow dock crane** that's been preserved from the old days. Nip across to the waterfront here for a final 'hidden' Granville Island view: a string of large and comfy-looking **houseboats** that many Vancouverites wish they lived in.

had been built and the Public Market quickly became an instantly popular anchor tenant. One reason for the island's popularity? Only independent, one-of-a-kind businesses operate here.

Twin Bridges

If you're out enjoying the buskers on the market's waterfront exterior, you'll notice your False Creek view is sandwiched between two of Vancouver's most famous bridges. Opened in 1954, the ironwork Granville Bridge is the third version of this bridge to span the inlet here. The more attractive art-deco Burrard Bridge, opened in 1932, is nearby. During its opening ceremony, a floatplane was daringly piloted under the bridge's main deck.

Walking Tour 🥾

Granville Island Artisan Trawl

Most visitors head straight for the Public Market but locals know there's much more to check out on this artificial island, built up from sandbanks in False Creek more than a century ago. The former industrial sheds are now home to crafty shops, studio spaces and cool theaters, inviting a leisurely waterfront exploration on sun-dappled days.

Walk Facts

Start Granville Island Licorice Parlour

End Granville Island Brewing

Length 1km; one hour

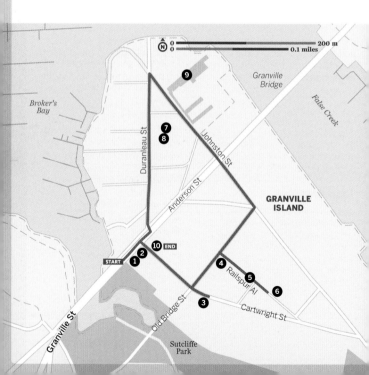

❶ Granville Island Licorice Parlour

Every stroll needs fuel, so drop into the friendly Granville Island Licorice Parlour (p94) for a hand-picked array of sweet and salty treats to keep you going.

❷ Kids Market

There's more than one market on the island and this one (p86) is fully focused on children. Look out for wooden toys, well-curated books and beady-eyed puppets.

❸ Crafthouse

There are dozens of artisan stores and gallery spaces to explore here but the red-painted Crafthouse (p95) is a one-stop shop for BC-made jewelry, woodwork and much more

❹ Liberty Distillery

Aim for Happy Hour at the saloon-look Liberty Distillery (p90) and you'll have the perfect pick-me-up. Don't overdo it, though, there's still plenty of walking to do.

❺ Railspur Alley

Starting just outside the distillery, this artisan-lined alleyway is a haven of creative businesses. Look out for inventive hats, eye-popping paintings and more.

❻ Artisan Sake Maker

In the middle of Railspur Alley, the Artisan Sake Maker (p90) is a welcoming little storefront where you can sample unique Vancouver-made libations. Consider buying a bottle to-go as well.

❼ Net Loft

Lined with intriguing boutiques, the Net Loft is ideal for discovering cool gifts for friends and family back home. Look for knitted toys, arts and crafts and local-made ceramics.

❽ Paper-Ya

The Net Loft's most popular store (p93) is home to an irresistible array of hip stationery, quirky books and must-have art prints.

❾ Public Market

Dominating the island's busy end, the market (p78) is a browser's paradise. But if you're hungry, you can also dive into tempting deli and bakery food stands.

❿ Granville Island Brewing

Toast your wander in the taproom of one of Vancouver's oldest breweries (p87). Or take the guided tour, samples included.

Yaletown & Granville Island

A
B
C
D

1

Nelson Park

Robson Sq

Jervis St
Comox St
Barclay St
Pendrell St
Nelson St
Davie St
Bute St
Burnaby St
Thurlow St
Harwood St

Sunset Beach Park

Seaside Promenade
Beach Ave
Pacific St
Burrard St
Hornby St
Howe St
Granville St
SkyTrain Canada Line

2

False Creek Ferry

Seymour St
Davie St
Helmcken St
Hamilton St

13 🍴

Burrard Bridge

Beach Ave
Drake St
Pacific St

10 🍴
Yaletown‑
Roundhouse

3

Seawall Trail

See Enlargement

7 🍴 Ⓢ
1 👁
Pacific Blvd
Engine 374 Pavilion

Broker's Bay

6 🍴

Granville Bridge

Granville Island

George Wainborn Park

David Lam Park

4

W 2nd Ave
11 🍴

Old Bridge St
Johnston St
Cartwright St

False Creek Ferry
Aquabus Ferry
False Creek

5

W 4th Ave

Granville St

Sutcliffe Park

The Mound

Spruce Harbour Marina

Fountain Way
Island Park Walk
Alder Bay

Charleson Park

FAIRVIEW
Lamey's Mill Rd
W 6th Ave

For reviews see	
👁 Top Experiences	p78
👁 Sights	p86
🍴 Eating	p87
✖ Drinking	p90
✪ Entertainment	p91
🔒 Shopping	p92

6

Oak St
W 7th Ave
Spruce St
W 8th Ave
Laurel St
W Broadway
Willow St

A
B
C
D

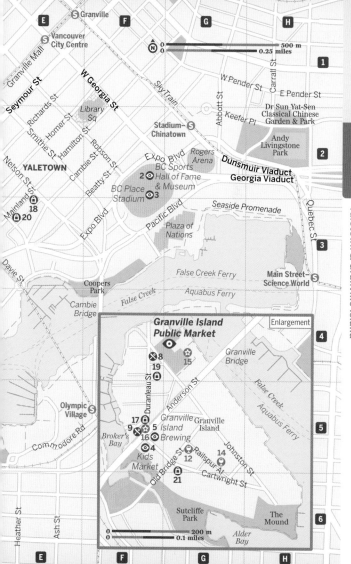

E

S Granville

Vancouver
City Centre

Granville Mall

Seymour St

Richards St

Smithe St

Nelson St

Homer St

YALETOWN

Hamilton St

Cambie St

Beatty St

Mainland St

🅐 18
🅐 20

Davie St

Coopers
Park

Cambie
Bridge

Olympic
Village S

Commodore Rd

Heather St

Ash St

F

W Georgia St

Library
Sq

Robson St

Expo Blvd

2 🅧 BC Sports
Hall of Fame
& Museum
BC Place
Stadium 🅧 3

Expo Blvd

Pacific Blvd

False Creek Ferry

False Creek

Aquabus Ferry

*Granville Island
Public Market*

🅧 8
19 🅐

Duranleau St

17 🅐
9 🅧 5
16 🅧
🅧 4
Kids
Market

Broker's
Bay

Old Bridge St

21 🅐

Sutcliffe
Park

0   200 m
0   0.1 miles

G

SkyTrain

Abbott St

W Pender St

Keefer St

Stadium–
Chinatown

Expo Blvd

Rogers
Arena

Plaza of
Nations

Anderson St

☆ 15

Granville
Bridge

Granville
Island

Granville
Island
Brewing

Railspur Al
12

Cartwright St

Johnston St

14

Alder
Bay

H

N 0
0   500 m
0.25 miles

Carrall St

E Pender St

Dr Sun Yat-Sen
Classical Chinese
Garden & Park

Andy
Livingstone
Park

Dunsmuir Viaduct
Georgia Viaduct

Quebec St

Seaside Promenade

Main Street–
Science World S

Enlargement

False Creek

Aquabus Ferry

The
Mound

1

2

3

4

5

6

Sights

Engine 374 Pavilion   MUSEUM

1 ◉ MAP P84, D3

May 23, 1887, was an auspicious date for Vancouver. That's when Engine 374 pulled the very first transcontinental passenger train into the fledgling city, symbolically linking the country and kick-starting the eventual metropolis. Retired in 1945, the engine was, after many years of neglect, restored and placed in this splendid pavilion. The friendly volunteers here will show you the best angle for snapping photos and share a few yesteryear railroading stories at the same time. (www.roundhouse.ca; 181 Roundhouse Mews, Roundhouse Community Arts & Recreation Centre, Yaletown; admission free; ⊘10am-4pm, reduced hours off-season; ᵻ; Ⓢ Yaletown-Roundhouse)

BC Sports Hall of Fame & Museum   MUSEUM

2 ◉ MAP P84, F2

Inside BC Place Stadium, this expertly curated attraction showcases top BC athletes, both amateur and professional, with an intriguing array of galleries crammed with fascinating memorabilia. There are medals, trophies and yesteryear sports uniforms on display (judging by the size of their shirts, hockey players were much smaller in the past), plus tons of hands-on activities to tire the kids out. Don't miss the **Indigenous**

Sport Gallery, covering everything from hockey to lacrosse to traditional Aboriginal games. (☏604-687-5520; www.bcsportshalloffame.com; 777 Pacific Blvd, Gate A, BC Place Stadium, Yaletown; adult/child $15/12; ⊘10am-5pm; ᵻ; Ⓢ Stadium-Chinatown)

BC Place Stadium   STADIUM

3 ◉ MAP P84, F2

Vancouver's main sports arena is home to two professional teams: the **BC Lions** Canadian Football League team and the **Vancouver Whitecaps** soccer team. Also used for international rugby sevens tournaments, major rock concerts and a wide array of consumer shows, the renovated stadium – with its huge, crown-like retractable roof – also hosted the opening and closing ceremonies for the 2010 Olympic and Paralympic Winter Games. (☏604-669-2300; www.bcplace.com; 777 Pacific Blvd, Yaletown; Ⓟ; Ⓢ Stadium-Chinatown)

Kids Market   MARKET

4 ◉ MAP P84, F5

A kaleidoscopic mini shopping mall for under-10s (there's even a special child-size entrance door), the Kids Market is crammed with 25 family friendly stores, mostly of the toy variety. If your child's interests extend beyond Lego, there are top-quality kites, books, puppets and educational wooden toys to consider here. Cool the sprogs down at the popular **Granville Island Water Park** (admission free;

May-Sep; 🚼; 🚌50) out back.
(📞604-689-8447; www.kidsmarket.
ca; 1496 Cartwright St, Granville Island;
🕐10am-6pm; 🚼; 🚌50)

Granville Island Brewing

BREWERY

5 🅾 MAP P84, F5

One of Canada's oldest micro-breweries (established in 1984), GIB offers short tours on which smiling guides walk you through the tiny brewing nook. The brewery has grown exponentially since opening and most of its beers are now made off-site, although some excellent small-batch brews are still made here on the island. The tour concludes with samples in the Taproom (p91). (📞604-687-2739; www.gib.ca; 1441 Cartwright St,

Granville Island; tours $11.50; 🕐tours
12:30pm, 2pm, 4pm & 5:50pm; 🚌50)

Eating

Go Fish

SEAFOOD $

6 🍴 MAP P84, A4

A short stroll westward along the seawall from the Granville Island entrance, this almost-too-popular seafood stand is one of the city's fave fish-and-chip joints, offering halibut, salmon and cod encased in crispy golden batter. The smashing fish tacos are also recommended, while changing daily specials – brought in by the nearby fishing boats – often include scallop burgers or ahi tuna sandwiches. (📞604-730-5040; 1505 W 1st Ave; mains $8-14; 🕐11:30am-6pm Mon-Fri, noon-6pm Sat & Sun; 🚌50)

Kids Market

Terry Fox, Canada's Hero

The most poignant gallery at the BC Sports Hall of Fame & Museum (p86) is dedicated to national legend Terry Fox, the young cancer sufferer whose one-legged 1980 Marathon of Hope run across Canada ended after 143 days and 5373km, when the disease spread to his lungs. Don't miss the memorial outside BC Place Stadium (p86), created by Vancouver artist and writer Douglas Coupland, who also penned a celebrated book, *Terry*, in tribute to Fox. The statue is a series of running figures showing Fox in motion during his cross-country odyssey. Every year since his death, fundraising runs have been held in Canada and around the world. The Terry Fox Foundation (www.terryfox.org) estimates these have raised more than $500 million for cancer research.

DD Mau
VIETNAMESE $

7 ✖ MAP P84, D3

At the forefront of Vancouver's love affair with Vietnamese banh mi sandwiches, this tiny, often-busy spot serves daily specials (always check these first) alongside five made-to-order regulars. Expect crisp baguette sandwiches (in large or half-order options) with diverse fillings including barbecue pork and lemongrass chicken. Seating is extremely limited so aim for takeout or visit its larger Chinatown branch. (☎604-684-4446; www.ddmau.ca; 1239 Pacific Blvd, Yaletown; sandwiches $5-13; ☺11am-4pm Mon-Sat; ☜; ⓈYaletown-Roundhouse)

A Bread Affair
BAKERY $

8 ✖ MAP P84, F4

A beloved Granville Island mainstay and must-visit for fans of great bread. Alongside its sandwich bar (French ham and Havarti recommended) plus racks of fresh-baked loaves, there's an irresistible array of treats, from cookies to croissants to rich chocolate brownies. Don't miss the hearty apple-cheddar-walnut galette; it's enough to feed two but that doesn't mean you have to. (☎604-695-0000; www.abreadaffair. com; 1680 Johnston St, Granville Island; sandwiches $8-12; ☺8:30am-7pm Mon-Thu, to 7:30pm Fri-Sun; 🚌50)

Tony's Fish & Oyster Cafe
SEAFOOD $$

9 ✖ MAP P84, F5

A chatty spot popular with both locals and visitors, this small, blue-checkered-tablecloth joint serves great fish and chips (cod, salmon or halibut), along with generous dollops of housemade coleslaw and tartar sauce. The food is good value, and it's not just about fish and chips; the BBQ-sauced oyster burger is almost a local legend. Service is fast and friendly. (☎604-683-7127; www.tonysfishandoystercafe.com; 1511 Anderson St, Granville Island; mains $11-23; ⏱11:30am-8pm Mon-Sat, to 7pm Sun; 🚌50)

MeeT
VEGAN $$

10 ⓧ MAP P84, D3

A hip vegan eatery that lures many carnivores with an array of meaty-seeming comfort-grub classics that emulate the flavors and textures of burgers, chicken and more. The Yaletown branch of this Vancouver minichain is often busy with chatty diners – which can mean waiting for peak-time tables. If you're starving, go for the bulging crispy barbecue burger or butter 'chicken' poutine. (☎604-696-1165; www.meetonmain.com; 1165

Mainland St, Yaletown; mains $10-17; ⏱11am-11pm Sun-Thu, to 1am Fri & Sat; ✒; Ⓢ Yaletown-Roundhouse)

Bistro 101
CANADIAN $$

11 ⓧ MAP P84, A4

The training restaurant of the Pacific Institute of Culinary Arts is a popular spot with in-the-know locals, especially at lunchtime, when $24 gets you a delicious three-course meal (typically three options for each course) alongside service that's earnestly solicitous. Dinner costs $8 more. There are also regular buffet options, typically on Fridays (lunch $28; dinner $38). Reservations are highly recommended. (☎604-734-4488; www.picachef.com; 1505 W 2nd Ave; prix fixe from $24; ⏱11:30am-1:15pm & 6-8:30pm Mon-Fri; 🚌50)

Terry Fox memorial

VOLODYMYR KYRYLYUK / SHUTTERSTOCK © ARTIST DOUGLAS COUPLAND

Yaletown & Granville Island Eating

Island's Best Fest

It might feel like an invasion but it's more accurate to call September's 11-day **Vancouver Fringe Festival** (www.vancouverfringe.com) an energetic occupation of Granville Island. The island's surfeit of theaters is well utilized, but shows are also staged at less conventional venues, from miniferries to pop-up street stages. Tickets are $12 to $15 but deals are plentiful and free shows are common: book ahead before you arrive.

Drinking

Liberty Distillery   DISTILLERY

12 🟢 MAP P84, G5

Gaze through internal windows at the shiny, steampunk-like booze-making equipment when you visit this handsome saloon-like tasting room. It's not all about looks, though. During happy hour (Monday to Thursday, 3pm to 6pm and after 8pm), sample housemade vodka, gin varieties and several whiskeys plus great $6 cocktails. Tours are also available ($10, 11:30am and 1:30pm Saturday and Sunday). (📞604-558-1998; www.thelibertydistillery.com; 1494 Old Bridge St, Granville Island; ⏱11am-9pm; 🚌50)

Small Victory   COFFEE

13 🟢 MAP P84, D3

The kind of austere, granite-countered coffee shop you might not feel cool enough to enter (or maybe that's just us), Small Victory is a favorite daytime hangout for hip Yaletowners. Sip your perfect cappuccino and standout flaky croissant (there's also an artful array of additional bakery treats) under the geometric wall-mounted artwork and you'll fit right in. (📞604-899-8892; www.smallvictory.ca; 1088 Homer St, Yaletown; ⏱7:30am-6pm Mon-Fri, 8am-6pm Sat & Sun; 🛜; Ⓢ Yaletown-Roundhouse)

Artisan Sake Maker   BREWERY

14 🟢 MAP P84, G5

Using locally grown rice, this tiny craft sake producer (the first of its kind in Canada) should be on everyone's Granville Island to-do list. Twinkle-eyed sake maker Masa Shiroki creates tempting tipples; you can dive in for a bargain $5 three-sake tasting. It's an eye-opening revelation to many drinkers who think sake is a harsh beverage. Takeout bottles also available. (📞604-685-7253; www.artisansakemaker.com; 1339 Railspur Alley, Granville Island; ⏱11:30am-6pm; 🚌50)

Granville Island Brewing Taproom PUB

At Granville Island Brewing (see 6 Map p84, F5) you can sample its beers in this often busy pub-style room, although most are now made in a far larger out-of-town facility. Of these, Cypress Honey Lager, Lions Winter Ale and False Creek Raspberry Ale are among the most popular. But the small-batch brews, made right here on the island, are even better; ask your server what's available. (604-687-2739; www.gib.ca; 1441 Cartwright St, Granville Island; noon-8pm; 50)

Entertainment

Vancouver Whitecaps SOCCER

Using BC Place Stadium (see 3 Map p84, F2) as its home, Vancouver's professional soccer team plays in North America's top-tier Major League Soccer (MLS). Their on-field fortunes have ebbed and flowed since being promoted to the league in 2011, but they've been finding their feet (useful for soccer players) lately. Save time to buy a souvenir soccer shirt to impress everyone back home. (604-669-9283; www.whitecapsfc.com; 777 Pacific Blvd, BC Place Stadium, Yaletown; tickets from $45; Mar-Oct; ; S Stadium-Chinatown)

Liberty Distillery

Yaletown & Granville Island Entertainment

Theater Tip

Granville Island is the heart of Vancouver's theater scene and hosts several stages. Savvy locals (and in-the-know visitors) save money on shows by checking the daily half-price deals at www.ticketstonight.ca.

BC Lions   FOOTBALL

Founded in 1954, the Lions is Vancouver's team in the Canadian Football League (CFL), which is arguably more exciting than its US counterpart, the NFL. Based at BC Place Stadium (see 3 ⊙ Map p84, F2), the team has had some decent showings lately, but hasn't won the all-important Grey Cup since 2011. Tickets are easy to come by – unless the boys are laying into their arch enemies, the Calgary Stampeders. (📞604-589-7627; www.bclions.com; 777 Pacific Blvd, BC Place Stadium, Yaletown; tickets from $20; ⊙Jun-Nov; 👫; Ⓢ Stadium-Chinatown)

Granville Island Stage   THEATER

15 ⭐ MAP P84, G4

The Granville Island arm of Vancouver's leading theater company, this intimate, raked-seating venue is the perfect spot to feel really connected to the action happening up on the stage. Cutting-edge homegrown shows as well as new versions of established hits popu-

late the season here and you're close to several restaurants if you fancy a dinner-and-show night out. (📞604-687-1644; www.artsclub.com; 1585 Johnston St, Granville Island; tickets from $29; ⊙Sep-Jun; 🚌50)

Vancouver Theatresports   COMEDY

16 ⭐ MAP P84, F5

The city's most popular improv group stages energetic romps – sometimes connected to themes like Tinder dating – at this purpose-built theater. Whatever the theme, the approach is the same: if you're sitting at one of the tables near the front, expect to be picked on. The late-night (11:15pm) shows are commendably ribald and probably not something to bring your parents to. (📞604-738-7013; www.vtsl.com; 1502 Duranleau St, Improv Centre, Granville Island; tickets from $15; ⊙Wed-Sun; 🚌50)

Shopping

Karen Cooper Gallery   ART

17 🔒 MAP P84, F5

You'll feel like you've entered a tranquil forest clearing when you open the door of this delightful nature-themed photography gallery. Cooper's striking work focuses on BC's jaw-dropping wild beauty, from coniferous trees to grizzly bears. Take your time and don't be surprised if you fall in love with a handsome image of a bald eagle perched on a mountain tree.

(☎604-559-5112; www.karencooper gallery.com; 1506 Duranleau St, Granville Island; ⊙10am-6pm, reduced hours winter; 🚌50)

Karameller Candy Shop

FOOD

18 🔒 MAP P84, E3

Grab a paper bag and some tongs then dive into the pick-your-own drawers of brightly colored treats at this slender, white-walled gem dedicated to Swedish candy. Among the 75 varieties, you'll find everything from caramel circles and mixed sour lips to peppermint licorice chalk and raspberry boats (the owner's favourite). Create a grab bag to go for your walk around Yaletown. (☎604-639-8325; www.karameller.com; 1020 Mainland St, Yaletown; ⊙11am-8pm Mon-Sat; Ⓢ Yaletown-Roundhouse)

Paper-Ya

ARTS & CRAFTS

19 🔒 MAP P84, F4

A magnet for all slavering stationery fetishists (you know who you are), this store's treasure trove of trinkets ranges from natty pens to traditional Japanese washi paper. It's not all writing-related ephemera, though. Whoever does the buying also curates an eclectic, changing roster of hard-to-resist goodies that can include cool journals, quirky books and cute greeting cards emblazoned with everything from cats to owls. (☎604-684-2531; www.paper-ya. com; 1666 Johnston St, Net Loft, Granville Island; ⊙10am-7pm Apr-Dec, to 6pm Jan-Mar; 🚌50)

BC Lions (with the ball) play Toronto Argonauts

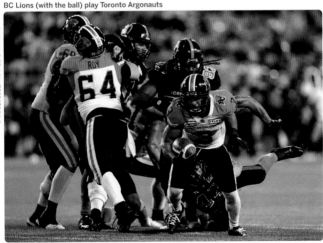

Vancouver's Brick-built SoHo

Railway Foundation

Aesthetically unlike any other Vancouver neighborhood, Yaletown has a trendy warehouse-district appearance today because it was built on a foundation of grungy, working-class history. Created almost entirely from red bricks, the area was crammed with railway sheds and goods warehouses in the late 1800s after the Canadian Pacific Railway (CPR) relocated its main western Canada operation from the British Columbia (BC) interior town of Yale.

Neighborhood Decline

Along with the moniker, the workers brought something else with them: a tough-as-nails, hard-drinking approach that turned the waterfront area into one where the taverns usually served their liquor with a side order of fist-fights. But at least the rough-and-ready workers kept the area alive: when the rail operations were closed down a few decades later, Yaletown descended into a half-empty mass squat filled with homeless locals and marauding rats.

Yaletown Rises

But that wasn't the end of the story. When plans were drawn up for Vancouver to host the giant **Expo '86** world exposition, there were few areas of town with the space – and the absence of other businesses – to host it. But Yaletown fit the bill. The area became part of the planned Expo grounds along the north shoreline of False Creek, and was cleared, refurbished and given a new lease on life.

Post-Expo Flourishing

After the summer-long fair, its newly noticed historic character made Yaletown the ideal spot for urban regeneration. Within a few years the old brick warehouses had been repaired, scrubbed clean and recolonized with a sparkling array of boutiques, fancy restaurants and swish bars serving tipples that are a far cry from the punch-triggering beers that used to be downed here.

Granville Island Licorice Parlour

FOOD

A satellite branch of Commercial Dr's popular candy store, this sweet-tooth pilgrimage spot at the Kids Market (see 4 ◉ Map p84, F5) serves up dozens of jars of serious licorice (anyone for salty *salmiak* from Scandinavia?) alongside a kaleidoscopic array of sweeties and bonbons such as jelly babies and saltwater taffy. There are also lots of gelatin-free and gluten-free options plus a supercool sideline

HARRY BEUGELINK / SHUTTERSTOCK ©

Yaletown streetscape

in brightly coloured Hula-Hoops. (📞604-428-0111; 1496 Cartwright St, Granville Island; 🕑10am-6pm; 🚌50)

Woo To See You

FASHION & ACCESSORIES

20 🔒 MAP P84, E3

Smiley, genuinely friendly service is the approach at this tiny womenswear boutique where you should give yourself plenty of time to browse the racks of carefully curated, independent labels. There's a Korean–Canadian fusion approach to the tops, jackets and pants on display, as well as a tempting selection of artisan jewelry that would please any passing magpie. (📞604-559-1062; www. wootoseeyou.com; 1061 Mainland St,

Yaletown; 🕑10am-7pm Mon-Sat, 11am-6pm Sun; 🚇Yaletown-Roundhouse)

Crafthouse

ARTS & CRAFTS

21 🔒 MAP P84, G5

At this bright and friendly nonprofit gallery run by the Craft Council of British Columbia (CCBC), the shelves hold everything from glass goblets and woven scarves to French butter dishes and lathe-turned arbutus wood bowls – all produced by dozens of artisans from across the region. It's a great place to pick up something different for friends and family back home. (📞604-687-7270; www.craftcouncil bc.ca; 1386 Cartwright St, Granville Island; 🕑10am-5:30pm; 🚌50)

Walking Tour 🚶

Commercial Drive
Beer & Bites

One of Vancouver's most historically eclectic neighborhoods, the Drive is lined with great places to hang with the locals on restaurant patios, in chatty bars and coffee shops and at independent stores and boutiques. It's also easy to get to and explore: a simple SkyTrain hop from downtown, the street unfolds just steps from the bustling Commercial-Broadway station.

Getting There

🚌 99B-Line express and regular bus 9 both stop at the intersection of Broadway and Commercial

🚈 Expo SkyTrain line from downtown to Commercial-Broadway station

❶ St Augustine's

Walk north from the SkyTrain station and you'll soon reach this busy **pub** (📞604-569-1911; www.staugustinesvancouver.com; 2360 Commercial Dr; 🕙11am-1am Sun-Thu, 11am-2am Fri & Sat; 📶; 🚇Commercial-Broadway), complete with dozens of tempting craft beers from BC and beyond.

❷ Prado

Sober up with the hip locals at **Prado** (📞604-255-5537; www.pradocafe.co; 1938 Commercial Dr; 🕙7am-8pm Mon-Fri, 7am-6pm Sat & Sun; 📶; 🚌20). It's one of many Drive coffee shops, testament to a rich java scene launched by Italian immigrants in the 1950s.

❸ Grandview Park

Time for a break? Sit on the grass at **Grandview Park** (Commercial Dr, btwn Charles & William Sts; 🚸; 🐾; 🚌20) while eyeballing the visuals to the north (craggy-topped peaks) and west (twinkling downtown towers).

❹ Biercraft Tap & Tapas

Next door's **BierCraft Tap & Tapas** (📞604-254-2437; www.biercraft.com; 1191 Commercial Dr; 🕙11am-midnight Mon-Thu, 11am-1am Fri, 10am-1am Sat, 10am-midnight Sun; 📶; 🚌20) has an enticing menu of local and imported beers. Alternatively, try a bowl of brothy, Belgian-style mussels.

❺ Sweet Cherubim

If you didn't eat at BierCraft, continue to **Sweet Cherubim** (📞604-253-0969; www.sweetcherubim.com; 1105 Commercial Dr; mains $7-12; 🕙10am-10pm Mon-Sat, 11am-10pm Sun; 📶🍴; 🚌20), where hearty vegan and vegetarian comfort food awaits.

❻ Licorice Parlour

Ready for dessert? The quirky **Licorice Parlour** (📞604-558-2422; 1002 Commercial Dr; 🕙11am-6pm Mon-Wed, 11am-6:30pm Thu-Sat, noon-6pm Sun; 🚌20) stocks imported varieties plus handmade Hula-Hoops (an ideal purchase unless your head is reeling from all that beer).

❼ East Van Brewing Company

Conclude your libation-loving wander with a tasting flight at **East Van Brewing Company** (📞604-558-3822; www.eastvanbrewing.com; 1675 Venables St; 🕙noon-11pm Sun-Thu, noon-midnight Fri & Sat; 📶; 🚌20), a local microbrewery favorite.

Explore

Main Street

Formerly faded and gritty, the skinny-jeaned heart of Vancouver's hipster scene is now its coolest 'hood, with many of its best independent shops, bars and restaurants. A great place to meet locals away from the city center, this area is developing rapidly. And that includes the Olympic Village, a waterfront neighborhood that's always adding new drinking and dining options.

The Short List

∘ *Regional Assembly of Text (p110)* Composing pithy missives to your loved one on vintage typewriters at the legendary monthly letter-writing club.

∘ *Anh & Chi (p104)* Dining on delightful contemporary Vietnamese dishes (and a glass or three of housemade punch) at this beloved restaurant.

∘ *Brassneck Brewery (p106)* Downing a Passive Aggressive pale ale at Vancouver's favorite neighborhood microbrewery.

∘ *Red Cat Records (p109)* Browsing the racks, buying local gig tickets and finally finding that signed Buttless Chaps album you've been looking for.

Getting There & Around

🚌 Number 3 runs the length of Main St in both directions.

🚈 SkyTrain connects to bus 3 services at Main St-Science World Station. If you're on the Canada Line, alight at Broadway-City Hall Station and take the 99B-Line bus along Broadway to Main St.

🚗 Limited metered parking on Main St, with side-street parking the further south you drive.

Main Street Map on p102

Olympic Village (p103) MEUNIERD / SHUTTERSTOCK ©
THE BIRDS BY MYFANWY MACLEOD (SCULPTOR).

Top Experience 📸
Entertain the Whole Family at Science World

Vancouver's landmark geodesic dome isn't just a shiny shoreline bauble; it's also home to the city's most popular family friendly attraction. Teeming with hands-on exhibits, engaging galleries, an eye-popping large-format movie theater and much more, it's the kind of attraction you plan to visit quickly but find yourself still exploring three hours later.

◉ MAP P102, B1

☏ 604-443-7440

www.scienceworld.ca

1455 Quebec St

adult/child $27.15/18.10

🕐 10am-6pm Jul & Aug, reduced hours off-season

P ⛹

S Main St-Science World

Ground Floor Fun

Start by letting your kids loose on the lower level's **Puzzles & Illusions** gallery, a tactile array of activities from wobble rings to whisper dishes. It's the kind of place your children will show you just how mush smarter they are than you. Reward their braininess by paying extra ($8) for **Birdly**, a virtual-reality solo flight over a tower-forested city. Nearby, take a seat and check out the schedule of live science demonstrations on the **Centre Stage**.

Head Upstairs

Next, wander up to the second level. It's circled by themed galleries bristling with hands-on action, including the nature-flavored **Sara Stern Gallery** (with fossils, taxidermy and live critters) and the brilliant **BodyWorks**, exploring the engineering marvels of the human body, with every fascinating function fully explained. This second level is where you'll likely spend much of your time; there's a huge array of imaginative exhibits here and your kids will likely become fully engaged in many of the options.

Go Outside

If the weather's fine, make sure you also save time for the outdoor **Ken Spencer Science Park**. Focused on sustainable communities, it's a quirky collection of climbing frames, rugged interactive games and stage demonstrations plus a coop-full of beady-eyed, brightly plumed chickens. Like a playground on steroids, many kids will happily spend hours here if you let them. But if it's time to leave, you can entice them away with a visit to Science World's popular gift shop, where excellent educational toys await.

★ Top Tips

o Omnimax movie screenings cost $12.75 but you can add one to your museum admission ticket for an extra $6.50.

o Check the times of Centre Stage shows when you arrive and plan your visit accordingly.

o After Dark adult evenings are very popular; book ahead online before you arrive.

o Add a miniferry cruise to your Science World day out; vessels dock nearby from Yaletown, Granville Island and other False Creek destinations.

✕ Take a Break

For a great finale to your family day out, head to Earnest Ice Cream (p103) for sit-down treats.

If dinner calls, walk around the False Creek shoreline to Tap & Barrel (p105), waterfront patio views included.

False Creek

Science World

Thornton Park

Pacific Central Station

Main Street–Science World

Olympic Village

Quebec St

Terminal Ave

MOUNT PLEASANT

Industrial Ave

Great Northern Way

Main St

W 1st Ave · E 1st Ave
W 2nd Ave
W 3rd Ave · E 3rd Ave
W 4th Ave · E 4th Ave
W 5th Ave · E 5th Ave
W 6th Ave · E 6th Ave

Alberta St · Columbia St · Ontario St

Jonathan Rogers Park

W 7th Ave · E 7th Ave
W 8th Ave · E 8th Ave
W Broadway · E Broadway
W 10th Ave · E 10th Ave
W 11th Ave · E 11th Ave
W 12th Ave · E 12th Ave

Scotia St · Brunswick St

Guelph Park

E Broadway

Guelph St · St George St · Carolina St · Fraser St · Prince Albert St

Alberta St · Manitoba St · Ontario St · Quebec St · Main St

W 13th Ave · E 13th Ave
W 14th Ave · E 14th Ave
W 15th Ave · E 15th Ave
W 16th Ave · E 16th Ave
W 17th Ave · E 17th Ave

Prince Edward St

Kingsway

Fraser St

W 18th Ave · E 18th Ave
W 19th Ave · E 19th Ave

SOUTH MAIN (SOMA)

E 20th Ave
W 20th Ave
W 21st Ave · E 21st Ave
W 22nd Ave · E 22nd Ave
W 23rd Ave · E 23rd Ave

Sophia St

E 24th Ave
W King Edward Ave · E King Edward Ave

Yukon St · Talismon St · Ontario St · Main St

Peveril Ave
E 26th St · E 26th Ave
E 27th St · E 27th Ave
E 28th Ave

500 m
0.25 miles

Sights

Olympic Village AREA

1 ◉ MAP P102, B1

Built as the home for 2800 athletes during the 2010 Olympic and Paralympic Winter Games, this glassy waterfront development became the city's newest neighborhood once the sporting types went home. Shops, bars and restaurants – plus some cool public art – have made this an increasingly happening area. Worth a look on your seawall stroll. (Athletes Way; S Main St-Science World)

Eating

Federal Store CAFE $

2 ✗ MAP P102, B3

Revitalizing an old corner store into a funky little community cafe, this warmly welcoming checker-floored charmer serves coffee, light breakfasts and delicious lunch sandwiches (go for the juicy porchetta). Among the bakery treats and a boutique array of artisan groceries and knickknacks, you'll feel like you're in the heart of the neighborhood among lots of chatty locals. (☎778-379-2605; www.federalstore.ca; 2601 Quebec St; mains $4-12; ◷8am-6pm; 🚌3)

Earnest Ice Cream ICE CREAM $

3 ✗ MAP P102, B2

The Olympic Village branch of this popular artisan ice-cream shop is tucked away in a redbrick former warehouse building. There's typically a dozen or so flavors, split between regulars including salted caramel and whiskey hazelnut plus seasonals such as the utterly delicious lemon poppy seed. All are available in cone or cup form – plus naughty to-go pint jars. (☎778-379-0697; www.earnesticecream.com; 1829 Quebec St; ice cream from $5; ◷10am-10pm; 🚌3)

Trafiq CAFE $

4 ✗ MAP P102, B6

A local favorite, this sometimes clamorously busy French-influenced bakery-cafe is a lunchtime magnet with its quesadillas, housemade soups and bulging grilled sandwiches (California club on cranberry pecan recommended). But the best time to come is off-peak when you can snag a table and take on one of the large, belly-busting cake slabs. Miss the salted-caramel slice at your peril. (☎604-648-2244; www.trafiq.ca; 4216 Main St; mains $7-10; ◷9am-6pm; 🍴; 🚌3)

Toshi Sushi JAPANESE $

5 ✗ MAP P102, B4

There are no reservations and the place is tiny, but this unassuming sushi joint just off Main is the best place in the neighborhood for Japanese dining. Expect to line up (try to arrive off-peak) before tucking into outstanding fresh-made dragon rolls, crunchy tempura and succulent sashimi platters; order a

Street Art Murals

Main Street and its tributaries are a walk-through kaleido-scope of eye-popping street art installations. The center of the annual **Vancouver Mural Festival** (www.vancouver muralfest.ca), dozens of strik-ing, richly colored works adorn the blank-canvas outer walls of large buildings here. Visit the festival's website for mural locations plus information on guided summer walks. Our favorites? We love the vivid creations on Industrial Ave and Southern St, between Western St and Station St.

selection and everyone at the table will be delighted. (📞604-874-5173; 181 E 16th Ave; mains $8-17; ⏰4:30-9:45pm Tue-Sat; 👶; 🚌3)

Anh & Chi   VIETNAMESE $$

6 🍴 MAP P102, B4

Warm and solicitous service wafts over you at this delightful contemporary Vietnamese res-taurant where authentic, perfectly prepared dishes make this a must for local foodies. Not sure what to order? Check out the menu's 'bucket list' dishes, including the highly recommended prawn-and-pork-packed crunchy crepe. Reservations are not accepted and waits here can be long; consider midafternoon weekday dining

instead. (📞604-878-8883; www. anhandchi.com; 3388 Main St; mains $16-25; ⏰11am-11pm; 🍴; 🚌3)

Acorn   VEGETARIAN $$

7 🍴 MAP P102, B6

One of Vancouver's hottest vegetarian restaurants – hence the sometimes long wait for tables – the Acorn is ideal for those craving something more inventive than mung-bean soup. Consider seasonal, artfully presented treats such as beer-battered haloumi or vanilla-almond-beet cake and stick around late-night: the bar serves until midnight if you need to pull up a stool and set the world to rights. (📞604-566-9001; www. theacornrestaurant.ca; 3995 Main St; mains $18-22; ⏰5:30-10pm Mon-Thu, to 11pm Fri, 10am-2:30pm & 5:30-11pm Sat, to midnight Sun; 🍴; 🚌3)

Dock Lunch   INTERNATIONAL $$

8 🍴 MAP P102, B3

Like dining in a cool hippie's home, this charming room in a side-street house serves a daily changing menu of one or two soul-food mains such as spicy tacos or heaping weekend brunches. Arrive early and aim for one of the two window seats and you'll soon be chatting with the locals or brows-ing the cookbooks and novels on the shelves. (📞604-879-3625; www. facebook.com/docklunch; 152 E 11th Ave; mains $10-18; ⏰noon-4pm Tue-Thu, noon-4pm & 7-10pm Fri, 11am-4pm Sat & Sun; 🚌3)

DARRYL BROOKS / SHUTTERSTOCK ©

Fish Counter

Fable Diner

DINER $$

9 ⊗ MAP P102, B3

Transforming a former greasy spoon diner in the landmark Lee Building into a casual satellite of Fable's popular Kitsilano restaurant, this hipster diner is a favorite hangout in Mount Pleasant. Settle yourself into a window booth or swivel chair at the kitchen-facing counter and dive into elevated all-day breakfasts and comfort grub, including dishes such as the smashing roast duck and kimchi pancake. (📞604-563-3463; www.fablediner. com; 151 E Broadway; mains $8-19; ⏰7:30am-10pm Mon-Thu, 7:30am-11pm Fri, 9:30am-11pm Sat, 9:30am-10pm Sun; 🛜🍴; 🚌9)

Fish Counter

SEAFOOD $$

10 ⊗ MAP P102, B5

Main's best fish and chips. This busy spot combines a seafood wet counter and a bustling fry operation. Order from the cashier, snag a spot at the stand-up table inside or sit-down benches outside and wait to be called. Battered halibut and cod are popular, but we love the wild salmon, served with fries and a mound of 'slaw. (📞604-876-3474; www.the fishcounter.com; 3825 Main St; mains $10-22; ⏰10am-8pm; 🚌3)

Tap & Barrel

NORTHWESTERN US $$

11 ⊗ MAP P102, B1

In the heart of Olympic Village, this popular neighborhood haunt serves gourmet comfort nosh such as Cajun chicken burgers and pineapple-and-pulled-pork pizzas but, in summer, it's all about the views from the expansive, mountain-facing waterfront patio (the area's best alfresco dining). Add some BC beer or wine and you'll have to be forcibly removed at the end of the night. (📞604-685-2223; www.tapandbarrel.com; 1 Athletes Way; mains $16-23; ⏰11am-midnight Mon-Sat, 10am-midnight Sun; 🚇Main St-Science World)

Drinking

Brassneck Brewery

MICROBREWERY

12 📍 MAP P102, B2

A beloved Vancouver microbrewery with a small, wood-lined tasting room. Peruse the ever-changing chalkboard of intriguing libations with names like Pinky Promise, Silent Treatment and Faux Naive or start with a delicious, highly accessible Passive Aggressive dry-hopped pale ale. It's often hard to find a seat here, so consider a weekday afternoon visit for a four-glass $8 tasting flight. (📞604-259-7686; www.brassneck.ca; 2148 Main St; ⏰2-11pm Mon-Fri, noon-11pm Sat & Sun; 🚌3)

Key Party

BAR

13 📍 MAP P102, B3

Walk through the doorway of a fake storefront that looks like an accountancy office and you'll find yourself in a candlelit, boudoir-red speakeasy dominated by a dramatic mural of frolicking women

Brassneck Brewery

Brewery Creek

Mainland Brewery, Red Star Brewery, San Francisco Brewery and, of course, Vancouver Brewery. The names of the city's long-gone beer producers recall a time when Brewery Creek (an area radiating from Main St around 7th Ave) concocted the suds quaffed by many ale-loving Vancouverites. The area was named after a fast-moving creek that once powered waterwheels at several area breweries. But after decades of consolidation, the neighborhood's last brewery closed in the 1950s. That wasn't the end of the story, though. Vancouver's latter-day craft brewing renaissance has seen several new producers open in this area, from **Main Street Brewing** to **33 Acres Brewing**. Wondering where to start? Slake your thirst at local favorite **Brassneck Brewery**.

and animals. Arrive early to avoid the queues, then fully explore the entertaining cocktail program (Kir Royale champagne jello shooters included). (www.keyparty.ca; 2303 Main St; ⏱5pm-1am Mon-Thu, to 2am Fri & Sat, to 1am Sun; 🚌3)

Shameful Tiki Room BAR

14 🚇 MAP P102, B6

This windowless snug instantly transports you to a Polynesian beach. The lighting – including glowing puffer-fish lampshades – is permanently set to dusk and the walls are lined with tiki masks and rattan coverings under a straw-shrouded ceiling. But it's the drinks that rock; seriously well-crafted classics from zombies to blue Hawaii's to a four-person Volcano Bowl (don't forget to share it). (www.shamefultikiroom.com; 4362 Main St; ⏱5pm-midnight Sun-Thu, to 1am Fri & Sat; 🚌3)

Kafka's COFFEE

15 🚇 MAP P102, B3

With more MacBooks than an Apple Store, locals fill the tables here silently updating their social media statuses as if their lives depended on it. But, despite appearances, this is a warm and welcoming hangout. The single-origin coffee is excellent and there's a serious commitment to local artworks on the walls; it's like quaffing in a cool gallery. (📞604-569-2967; www.kafkascoffee.ca; 2525 Main St; ⏱7am-10pm Mon-Thu, 7am-8pm Fri, 8am-8pm Sat & Sun; 📶; 🚌3)

Narrow Lounge BAR

16 🚇 MAP P102, B2

Enter through the doorway on 3rd Ave – the red light tells you if it's open or not – then descend the graffiti-lined stairway into one of Vancouver's coolest small bars.

Dancers celebrating Car Free Day

Little bigger than a train carriage and lined with taxidermy and junk-shop pictures, it's an atmospheric nook that always feels like 2am. In summer, try the hidden alfresco bar out back. (☎778-737-5206; www.narrowlounge.com; 1898 Main St; �spm-1am Mon-Fri, to 2am Sat & Sun; ☐3)

Sing Sing Beer Bar BAR

17 📍 MAP P102, B3

This bright, white-walled, plant-accented bar would look at home on a Singapore side street. Snag a communal table and dive into the 20 or so BC craft beer taps (often including lesser-known libations from celebrated microbreweries such as Twin Sails and Fuggles & Warlock). Food-wise, there's an unusual combination of pizzas and hearty pho bowls on the menu. (☎604-336-9556; www.singsingbeer bar.com; 2718 Main St; ☐11am-1am; ☎; ☐3)

Gene Cafe COFFEE

18 📍 MAP P102, B3

Colonizing a flatiron wedge of bare concrete floors and oversized windows, locals treat Gene as their living room hangout, especially if they manage to monopolize one of the three tiny tables overlooking Main and Kingsway. Coffee is art-fully prepared and the menu has expanded to include flaky croissants (gooey chocolate variety recommended) plus Aussie-style meat pies and all-day breakfast wraps. (☎604-568-5501; http://genecoffeebar.com; 2404 Main

St; ⏱7:30am-7pm Mon-Fri, 8:30am-7pm Sat & Sun; ☎; 🚌3)

Entertainment

Fox Cabaret
LIVE MUSIC

One of North America's last-remaining porn cinemas has been transformed (and fully pressure-washed) into a brilliantly eclectic independent nightlife venue, ditching the dodgy flicks in favor of live bands, rib-tickling comedy and Saturday night dance fests with disco or '90s themes. There's always something different on stage in this narrow, high-ceilinged venue located just a couple of doors down from cocktail bar Key Party (see 13 🍸 Map p102, B3). Check the online calendar. (www.foxcabaret.com; 2321 Main St; 🚌3)

Main Street's Best Fest

If you make it to the neighborhood's annual **Car Free Day** (www.carfreevancouver.org), staged along Main St from the Broadway intersection for at least 30 blocks, you'll realize there's much more diversity in this area than you thought. Taking over the streets for this family friendly community event are live music, craft stalls, steaming food stands and a highly convivial atmosphere that make for a brilliant party-like afternoon with the locals.

BMO Theatre Centre
THEATER

19 ⭐ MAP P102, A1

The studio venue of the city's Arts Club theater empire hosts more challenging and intimate productions in a space that's cleverly and sometimes dramatically reconfigured for each show. There are often three or four productions per season as well as on-stage readings of new works in progress, which are typically free; check the Arts Club website for information on these. (📞604-687-1644; www.artsclub.com; 162 W 1st Ave; tickets from $29; 🚌3)

Biltmore Cabaret
LIVE MUSIC

20 ⭐ MAP P102, C3

One of Vancouver's favorite alt venues, the intimate Biltmore is a firm fixture on the local indie scene. A low-ceilinged, good-vibe spot to mosh to local and touring musicians, it also has regular event nights; check the online calendar for upcoming happenings, including trivia nights and stand-up comedy shows. (📞604-676-0541; www.biltmorecabaret.com; 2755 Prince Edward St; tickets from $15; 🚌9)

Shopping

Red Cat Records
MUSIC

21 🔒 MAP P102, B6

Arguably Vancouver's coolest record store and certainly the only one named after a much-missed cat... There's a brilliantly curated collection of new and used vinyl and CDs, and it's co-owned by musicians; ask them for tips on where to see great local acts such as Loscil and Nick Krgovich or peruse the huge list of shows in the window. (☎604-708-9422; www. redcat.ca; 4332 Main St; ☉11am-7pm Mon-Thu, to 8pm Fri & Sat, to 6pm Sun; 🚇3)

Regional Assembly of Text
ARTS & CRAFTS

22 🔒 MAP P102, B6

This ironic antidote to the digital age lures ink-stained locals with its journals, handmade pencil boxes and T-shirts printed with typewriter motifs. Check out the tiny under-the-stairs gallery showcasing global zines, and don't miss the monthly Letter Writing Club (7pm, first Thursday of every month), where you can hammer on vintage typewriters, crafting erudite missives to far-away loved ones. (☎604-877-2247; www.assembly oftext.com; 3934 Main St; ☉11am-6pm Mon-Sat, noon-5pm Sun; 🚇3)

Urban Source
ARTS & CRAFTS

23 🔒 MAP P102, B4

From used postcards and insect rubber stamps to ladybug stickers and map pages from old books, this brilliant store offers a highly eclectic, ever-changing array of reclaimed materials and alternative arts-and-crafts supplies to a loyal band of locals. In this browser's paradise you'll suddenly be inspired to make an oversized pterodactyl model from glitter

Red Cat Records (p109)

JOHN LEE / LONELY PLANET ©

and discarded cassette tapes.
(📞604-875-1611; www.urbansource.
bc.ca; 3126 Main St; ⏰10am-5:30pm
Mon-Sat, 11am-5:30pm Sun; 👪; 🚌3)

Front & Company
CLOTHING

24 🔒 MAP P102, B5

You could easily spend a couple
of hours perusing the new and
vintage clothing in the main space
of Front & Company, which colo-
nizes a row of storefronts along
Main and threatens to become a
hipster department store in the
process. There's also knowingly
cool housewares and must-have
gifts and accessories (anyone for
manga nightlights and unicorn
ice trays?). (📞604-879-8431; www.
frontandcompany.ca; 3772 Main St;
⏰11am-6:30pm; 🚌3)

Smoking Lily
CLOTHING

25 🔒 MAP P102, B5

Art-school-cool rules at this
mostly womenswear boutique,
with skirts, belts and halter tops
whimsically accented with prints
of rabbits, narwhals and the
periodic table. Anatomically cor-
rect heart motifs are also popular,
appearing on shirts, jewelry and
cushion covers. And there's a great
array of accessories, including
quirky purses and shoulder bags
beloved of the local pale-and-
interesting set. (📞604-873-5459;
www.smokinglily.com; 3634 Main St;
⏰10:30am-6:30pm Mon-Sat, noon-
5pm Sun; 🚌3)

Neptoon Records
MUSIC

26 🔒 MAP P102, B5

Vancouver's oldest independent
record store is still a major lure for
music fans, with its *High Fidelity*
ambience and time-capsule feel.
But it's not resting on its laurels:
you'll find a well-priced array of
new and used vinyl and CD recordings, plus some serious help with
finding that obscure Mighty Wah!
recording you've been looking for.
(📞604-324-1229; www.neptoon.com;
3561 Main St; ⏰11am-6:30pm Mon-
Sat, noon-5pm Sun; 🚌3)

Mintage Mall
VINTAGE

27 🔒 MAP P102, B3

Comprising seven vintage vendors
offering everything from 1970s
outfits (at Thirteen Moons) to antique taxidermy (Salamander Salt
Curio), this eclectic, labyrinthine
upstairs 'mall' is one of the best
ways to spend an hour in Mount
Pleasant. Don't miss the ever-
changing pop-up unit, add a tarot
reading to keep things lively and
check out its Instagram account
for after-hours events. (📞604-428-
6732; 245 E Broadway; ⏰11am-7pm
Mon-Sat, to 6pm Sun; 🚌9)

Bird on a Wire Creations
ARTS & CRAFTS

Specializing in BC artisans,
there's an eminently browsable
and surprisingly diverse array of
tasteful handmade goodies at this
ever-friendly store situated next
to Kafka's coffee shop (see 15 🔘

Vancouver's Summer Fair

One annual family-friendly Vancouver event is still going strong after more than a century. Launched in 1912, the **Pacific National Exhibition** (www.pne.ca) – known simply as the PNE by locals – is an August tradition for generations of Vancouverites. It's held in East Vancouver; you can reach it by hopping onboard the number 14 bus at the intersection of Main and Hastings Sts.

Planning your Visit

Arrive as close to opening time as you can. This helps beat the crowds but also gives you the chance to see as much as possible. The site is crammed with **exhibition halls** and **arenas**; take time to check out the **market halls** lined with vendors selling 'miracle' made-for-TV products. Then head to the **livestock barns**; the PNE is an important agricultural show for BC farmers, and these barns are lined with prize horses, cows, goats and sheep.

Daily Shows

Included with your admission (typically around $18 but cheaper if bought via the PNE website) is a wide array of other performances running all day. These have included **magician shows**, **motorcycle stunts** and the **SuperDogs**. There's also **live music** on alfresco stages throughout the day, especially in the evening, with nostalgic acts such as Foreigner and Smokey Robinson adding to the party atmosphere.

Midway Shenanigans

The site's **Playland fairground** offers more than 50 rides, ranging from dodgems to horror houses, but the top lure for thrillseekers is the 1950s-built wooden **roller coaster**. Coaster aficionados from across North America frequently eulogize this scream-inducing boneshaker, which reaches speeds of up to 75km (47 miles) an hour.

Street Food Heaven

This is also the one time of year when Vancouverites forget about their health regimen, happily stuffing themselves silly. The midway is jam-packed with naughty treats from **deep-fried ice-cream** to **two-foot-long hotdogs**. And don't miss the event's biggest diet-defying tradition: warm bags of sugar-coated **minidonuts**.

GARETH JANZEN / SHUTTERSTOCK ©

Pacific National Exhibition

Map p102, B3). Check out the cute jewelry, artsy T-shirts, ceramic tea tankards and fiber arts kids' toys (that adults want, too). But it's not just for show; there are regular craft classes here, too. (604-874-7415; www.birdonawirecreations.com; 2535 Main St; 10am-6pm Mon-Sat, 11am-5pm Sun; 3)

Pulpfiction Books
BOOKS

28 MAP P102, B3

One of the city's best used-book stores (there are also plenty of new tomes in the front room), this is the ideal haunt for the kind of serious browsing where you forget what time it is. You'll find good literature and sci-fi sections, as well as a travel area at the back for planning your next big trip. (604-876-4311; http://pulpfictionbooksvancouver.com/; 2422 Main St; 10am-8pm Mon-Wed, 10am-9pm Thu-Sat, 11am-7pm Sun; 3)

Explore
Fairview & South Granville

Combining the boutiques and restaurants of well-to-do South Granville with Fairview's busy Broadway thoroughfare and cozy Cambie Village, there's something for everyone in this area. It's a great spot to scratch beneath the city's surface and meet the locals where they live, shop and socialize. Green-thumbed visitors should also save time for some top-notch park and garden attractions here.

The Short List

○ **Bloedel Conservatory (p122)** *Spotting rainbow-hued tropical birds, then discovering the surrounding park's panoramic city views.*

○ **Pacific Arts Market (p128)** *Perusing the work of dozens of regional artists and artisans in this shared gallery space.*

○ **Vij's (p125)** *Faceplanting into Vancouver's (and maybe Canada's) finest Indian food; lamb popsicles included.*

Getting There & Around

🚇 Cambie Village's shopping and dining area is sandwiched between the Canada Line SkyTrain stations at Broadway-City Hall and King Edward. The rest of Fairview also radiates along Broadway from the Broadway-City Hall station.

🚌 Service 15 runs along Cambie St; bus 10 along South Granville. The two streets are linked along Broadway by bus numbers 9 and 99B-Line express.

🚗 There is metered parking on Cambie and South Granville.

Fairview & South Granville Map on p120

City Hall (p123) PETERSPIRO / GETTY IMAGES ©

Top Experience 📷
Watch Eagles and Turtles in VanDusen Botanical Garden

Vancouver's favorite manicured green space is a delightful confection of verdant walkways fringed by local and exotic flora. Just wandering around the mirror-calm lake is enough to slow your heart rate to tranquility levels – a useful reminder that there's more to the world than your cellphone screen. Don't throw it in the water, though; you'll need it to snap photos.

◎ MAP P120, B8

www.vandusengarden.org

5151 Oak St

adult/child Apr-Sep $11.25/5.50

⏱ 9am-8pm Jun-Aug, to 6pm Apr & Sep, to 7pm May, reduced hrs Oct-Mar

🚌 17

Plant Life

Opened in 1975, this 22-hectare (55-acre) green-thumbed wonderland is home to more than 250,000 plants representing some of the world's most distinct growing regions. You'll find trees, shrubs, flowers, succulents and more from across Canada, the Mediterranean, South Africa and the Himalayas, many of them identified with little plaques near their roots. There's almost always something in bloom here; if you're lucky, that might include the eye-popping **Rhododendron Walk** or neon-yellow, tunnel-like **Laburnum Walk**. Pick up a self-guided tour sheet from the front desk for seasonal tips on what to see or time your visit for a free guided tour.

Wildlife

It's not just humans that are hooked by this sparkling nature swathe; this is also a wildlife haven. Look out for turtles, herons and a variety of ducks in and around the main lake. You might also see owls, bats, raccoons or the occasional coyote in quiet corners. But birds are the main creatures here. There are regular guided bird walks (included with admission), and highlights that lure visiting camera lenses include eagles, hummingbirds and woodpeckers.

Elizabethan Maze

Grown from more than 3000 pyramidal cedars, VanDusen's traditional maze is the perfect spot to tire out your kids. Alternatively, just send them in there alone while you take a break outside. Laid out and planted in 1981, the maze has just the right combination of confusing dead-ends and gratifying solvability to give most visitors an entertaining diversion.

★ Top Tips

o Quiz the docents. These wandering volunteers are a font of knowledge about what plants and wildlife to spot during your visit.

o VanDusen is also studded with art-works; see how many you can spot along the walkways.

o The **Garden Shop** is stuffed with excellent books and gifts for the botanically inclined.

o VanDusen's **Festival of Lights** is a Christmas tradition with thousands of twinkling bulbs dotting the gardens.

✖ Take a Break

Head to VanDusen's **Truffles Cafe** (☎604-505-4961; www.trufflesfinefoods. com; mains $6-12; ⏰8:30am-8pm, reduced hours low season; ✍) for light lunches and fair-trade coffee. We recommend a patio table facing the garden.

Walking Tour 🥾

South Granville Stroll

Once the only independent gallery district in the city (there are still more than a few to peruse here), South Granville is now better known as an outdoor shopping promenade that's well worth a stroll and a browse. There's plenty to consider buying, plus plenty of places to stop for a fuel-up or a more substantial meal.

Walk Facts

Start Paul's Omelettery
End Bump n Grind
Length 1.5km; one hour

❶ Paul's Omelettery

On the right side of Granville St, just past the south end of the bridge, Paul's Omelettery (p123) is a legend among breakfast-loving locals. Dive into a heaping plate and then work it off as you speed-walk uphill.

❷ Pacific Arts Market

Take the stairs to this friendly, well-hidden 2nd-floor spot (p128) and you'll discover a cornucopia of arts and crafts created by an ever-changing array of BC creative types. Looking for unique souvenirs? You'll find everything from painted ceramics to handmade chocolate bars here.

❸ Purdy's Chocolates

If you didn't find any chocolate at the market, drop by Purdy's (p129), an historic, homegrown confectionary chain with purple-hued branches throughout the region. Pick up some treats for later or an ice-cream bar for the road.

❹ Rangoli

You'll have spotted lots of enticing restaurants on your walk, covering cuisines from Japanese to Lebanese to vegetarian. But if you're starting to seriously consider your dinner options, check out the menu at this tasty modern Indian restaurant (p124).

❺ Stanley Theatre

Just around the corner, this handsome heritage theater (p127) is one of the city's most popular performance venues. Check to see what's on and consider booking tickets for an evening show.

❻ Bacci's

This stretch of South Granville is lined on both sides with tempting boutiques but this well-curated store (p129) should be on everyone's shopping list. Check out the funky home wares and trendy fashions here.

❼ Meinhardt Fine Foods

Not far from the area's posh Shaughnessy neighborhood, Meinhardt Fine Foods (p129) is a high-end Vancouver deli and grocery store. Explore the aisles of fancy goods and tempting treats here.

❽ Bump n Grind

If all that walking has your blisters throbbing, rest your weary feet at Bump n Grind (p125), a cool coffee shop with a cabinet full of baked treats. Alternatively, head straight for dinner at one of the places you picked out along the way.

Fairview & South Granville

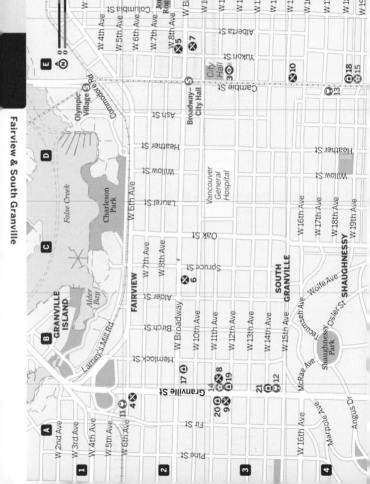

Map Labels

W 20th Ave
W 21st Ave
W 22nd Ave
W 23rd Ave
Ontario St

Manitoba St
Peveril Ave
Hillcrest Park
16 Nat Bailey Stadium
W King Edward Ave
Midlothian Ave
Dumfries Ave
Yukon St
Talisman St
2
Queen Elizabeth Park
Bloedel Conservatory
1
SkyTrain Canada Line
King
S Edward
Cambie St
Kersland Dr
W 26th Ave
W 27th Ave
W 28th Ave
W 29th Ave
W 33rd Ave
Heather St
W 37th Ave

W 20th Ave
Douglas Park
W 22nd Ave
W 23rd Ave
W 24th Ave
Laurel St
Braemar Park
CAMBIE
Oak St
Osler St
Selkirk St
BC Children's Hospital
Willow St
Oak St

Hudson St
W King Edward Ave
W 26th Ave
Nanton Ave
Devonshire Cr
Devonshire Park
Connaught Dr
W 32nd Ave
Granville St
VanDusen Botanical Garden

Matthews Ave
Balfour Ave
Laurier Ave
W King Edward Ave
W 26th Ave
W 28th Ave
W 29th Ave
W 33rd Ave
Alexandra St
Beverly Cres

For reviews see	
Top Experiences	p116
Sights	p122
Eating	p123
Drinking	p125
Entertainment	p127
Shopping	p128

Sights

Bloedel Conservatory

GARDENS

1 ◉ MAP P120, E7

Cresting the hill in Queen Elizabeth Park, this domed conservatory is a delightful rainy-day warm-up. Vancouver's best-value paid attraction, you'll find tropical trees and plants bristling with hundreds of free-flying, bright-plumaged birds. Listen for the noisy resident parrots but also keep your eyes peeled for rainbow-hued Gouldian finches, shimmering African superb starlings and maybe even a dramatic Lady Amherst pheasant, snaking through the undergrowth. Ask nicely and the attendants might even let you feed the smaller birds from a bowl. (☎604-257-8584; www.vandusengarden.org; 4600 Cambie St, Queen Elizabeth Park; adult/child $6.75/3.30; ⏰10am-5pm Jan-Mar, Nov & Dec, 10am-6pm Apr, Sep & Oct, 10am-8pm May-Aug; 🅿🚻; 🚌15)

Queen Elizabeth Park

PARK

2 ◉ MAP P120, E7

The city's highest point – it's 167m above sea level and has panoramic views over the mountain-framed downtown skyscrapers – this 52-hectare park claims to house specimens of every tree native to Canada. Sports fields, manicured lawns and formal gardens keep the locals happy, and you'll likely also see wide-eyed

Bloedel Conservatory

MR.NIKON / SHUTTERSTOCK ©

Behind the Deco Facade

The Great Depression caused major belt-tightening among regular folks in 1930s Vancouver. But despite the economic malaise, mayor Gerry McGeer spared no expense to build a new **City Hall** in 1936. Defended as a make-work project for the idled construction industry, the $1 million project (a huge sum for the time) was completed in just 12 months. Despite the controversy, the building is now one of Vancouver's most revered art deco edifices, complete with a soaring, Gotham-style exterior and an interior of streamlined signs, cylindrical lanterns and embossed elevator doors.

couples posing for their wedding photos in particularly picturesque spots. A good place to view local birdlife, be on the look out for chickadees, hummingbirds and huge bald eagles whirling high overhead. (www.vancouverparks.ca; entrance cnr W 33rd Ave & Cambie St; P; 🚌15)

City Hall
HISTORIC BUILDING

3 ◎ MAP P120, E3

Architecture fans should save time for one of Vancouver's best art-deco buildings. Snap some photos of the statue of Captain George Vancouver outside, then check out the handsome wooden heritage mansions on surrounding Yukon St and W 12th Ave. Finally, snag a table at the public plaza next to City Hall for some grand mountain-framed cityscape views. (📞604-873-7000; www.vancouver.ca; 453 W 12th Ave, Fairview; admission free; ⊙8:30am-5pm Mon-Fri; P; S Broadway-City Hall)

Eating

Paul's Omelettery
BREAKFAST $

4 ✖ MAP P120, A2

You'll be jostling for space with chatty locals at this breakfast and lunch joint near the south side of Granville Bridge. But it's worth it: the cozy, superfriendly place is superior to most bacon-and-eggs destinations. The menu is grounded on signature omelets, while also offering excellent eggs Benedict and heaping 'lumber-jack breakfasts.' Reservations are not accepted; arrive early on weekends. (📞604-737-2857; www.paulsomelettery.com; 2211 Granville St, South Granville; mains $6-19; ⊙7am-3pm; 🍴; 🚌10)

La Taquería Pinche Taco Shop
MEXICAN $

5 ✖ MAP P120, E2

The latest finger-licking edition of this wildly popular Mexican

Christmas in Vancouver

From mid-November onwards, dozens of Yuletide offerings pop up around the city, from seasonal markets to festive stage shows to a giant annual parade. One of the best places to tap into the Christmas spirit is VanDusen Botanical Garden (p116), which transforms into a colorful winter wonderland of fairy lights and sparkling dioramas. Considering a festive city visit? See what else is on at www.vancouverchristmas guide.com.

minichain combines communal tables, a large patio and an inviting bar area with a full menu of favorites, Order a selection of meat and/or veggie tacos for the table (*al pastor* and *asada* recommended) and add some beers from Vancouver-based South American brewery Andina. Ask about afternoon and late-night happy-hour specials here. (☎604-558-2549; www.lataqueria.com; 2450 Yukon St, Fairview; tacos $3-6; mains $14-17; ⏲11am-11pm Mon-Thu, 11am-midnight Fri & Sat, 11am-9pm Sun; ☏; ☐9)

Salmon n' Bannock

NORTHWESTERN US $$

6 ⊗ MAP P120, C2

Vancouver's only First Nations restaurant is an utterly delightful art-lined little bistro on an unassuming strip of Broadway shops. It's worth the easy bus trip, though, for fresh-made aboriginal-influenced dishes made with local ingredients. The juicy salmon n' bannock burger has been a staple here for years but more elaborate, feast-like options include game sausages and bison pot roast. (☎604-568-8971; www.facebook. com/SalmonNBannockBistro; 1128 W Broadway, Fairview; mains $16-32; ⏲5-10pm Mon-Sat; ☐9)

Heritage Asian Eatery

ASIAN $$

7 ⊗ MAP P120, E2

Bigger than its Pender St sister restaurant, this bright, cafeteria-style spot serves a small, well-curated menu of comfort food rice-and-noodle bowls. Focused on top-notch ingredients such as velvety pork belly and spicy lamb shank, there's also a couple of flavor-hugging vegetarian options; go for the lip-smacking eggplant rice bowl. On your way out, add a warm egg custard bun to your day. (☎604-559-6058; www.eatheritage.ca; 382 W Broadway, Fairview; mains $12-18; ⏲11am-8pm; ☏✶; ☐9)

Rangoli

INDIAN $$

8 ⊗ MAP P120, B3

This small, cafe-like satellite of the Cambie St landmark Vij's restaurant is a favorite among South Granville locals. Service is brisk and famously friendly and the menu takes a gourmet-comfort-food approach to Indian dishes such as the delicious lamb in cumin-and-cream curry. Add some addictive pakoras to share but make sure you snag the last one for yourself. (📞604-736-5711; www.vijsrangoli.ca; 1480 W 11th Ave, South Granville; mains $16-32; ⏱11:30am-1am Sun-Thu, 11:30am-2am Fri & Sat; 🖋; 🚌10)

Heirloom Vegetarian
VEGETARIAN $$

9 🍴 MAP P120, A3

With a white-walled cafeteria-meets-rustic-artisan look (hence the farm forks on the wall), this is one of Vancouver's best vegetarian eateries, serving mostly BC and organic seasonal ingredients fused with international influences. Dinner-wise, the bulging burger and cashew coconut curry are winners but the all-day brunch has risen to prominence, especially the delicious avocado eggs benny. (📞604-733-2231; www.heirloomrestaurant.ca; 1509 W 12th Ave, South Granville; mains $11-22; ⏱9am-10pm; 🖋; 🚌10)

Vij's
INDIAN $$$

10 🍴 MAP P120, E4

Spicy aromas scent the air as you enter this warmly intimate dining space for Vancouver's finest Indian cuisine. Exemplary servers happily answer menu questions, while bringing over snacks and spiced chai. There's a one-page array of tempting dishes but the trick is to order three or four to share (mains are all available as small plates and orders are accompanied with rice and naan). (📞604-736-6664; www.vijs.ca; 3106 Cambie St, Cambie Village; mains $23-36; ⏱5:30-10pm; 🖋; 🚌15)

Drinking

Grapes & Soda
WINE BAR

11 🚇 MAP P120, A1

A warm, small-table hangout that self-identifies as a 'natural wine bar' (there's a well-curated array of options from BC, Europe and beyond), this local favorite also serves excellent cocktails. From the countless bottles behind the small bar, they can seemingly concoct anything your taste buds desire, whether or not it's on the menu. Need help? Slide into a Scotch, ginger and walnut Cortejo. (📞604-336-2456; www.grapesandsoda.ca; 1541 W 6th Ave, South Granville; ⏱5:30-11pm Tue-Sat; 🚌10)

Bump n Grind
COFFEE

12 🚇 MAP P120, A3

The South Granville branch of this two-outlet local coffee chain has a great long table at the back where you can settle down with a java and peruse the tiny wall-mounted library of zines. Alternatively, press your face against the glass cabinet of bakery treats at the front and try to levitate a muffin or cookie into your mouth. (📞604-558-4743; www.bumpngrindcafe.com; 3010 Granville St, South Granville; ⏱7am-7pm Mon-Fri, 8am-7pm Sat & Sun; 📶; 🚌10)

Vancouver
Animal Watch

Common Critters

Vancouver's urban green spaces are home to a surprising array of critters. Many of them roam the city's streets after dark, foraging for extra food.

During your visit, you'll find **black squirrels** everywhere, but don't be surprised to also spot **raccoons**. Common in several parks, they are often bold enough to hang out on porches and root through garbage bins. **Skunks** are almost as common, but the only time you'll likely see them is after an unfortunate roadkill incident (a fairly common occurrence around area parks).

But while squirrels, raccoons and skunks are regarded as urban nuisances, some animals in the city are much larger.

Bigger Critters

Every spring, several Vancouver neighborhoods post notices of **coyote** spottings (there are an estimated 3000 living in and around the city). This is the time of year when these wild dogs build dens and raise pups, often in remote corners of city parks – and they become more protective of their territory in the process. This can lead to problems with domesticated pets.

Vancouverites are warned to keep pets inside when coyotes are spotted in their neighborhoods, and report any sightings to authorities. Many locals will tell you they've only seen a coyote once or twice; these animals are very adept at avoiding humans.

Animal Encounters

Human–animal interactions are an even bigger problem for areas that back directly on to wilderness regions. The North Shore is shadowed by a forest and mountain swathe that's long been a traditional home for **bears** – mostly black bears. Residents in North Vancouver and West Vancouver know how to secure their garbage so as not to encourage bears to become habituated to human food. But every year – often in spring when the hungry furballs are waking from hibernation – a few are trapped and relocated from the area.

For more information on wildlife (and guided nature walks) in the city, click on www.stanleyparkecology.ca.

BierCraft Bistro

BEER HALL

13 📞 MAP P120, E4

With a chatty, wood-lined interior plus two popular street-side patios, this beer-forward resto-bar is a great spot for ale aficionados. Dive into the astonishing array of Belgian tipples and compare them to some choice microbrews from BC and the US. Save time for food; the slightly pricey gastropub menu here ranges from steak *frites* to bowls of locally sourced mussels in several brothy iterations. (📞604-874-6900; www.biercraft.com; 3305 Cambie St, Cambie Village; ⏱11:30am-midnight Mon-Thu, 11:30am-1am Fri, 10am-1am Sat, 10am-midnight Sun; 🚌15)

Nat Bailey Stadium (p128)

Entertainment

Stanley Theatre

THEATER

14 ⭐ MAP P120, A3

Popular musicals dominate early summer at this heritage theater, but the rest of the year sees new works and adaptations of contemporary hits from around the world. Officially called the Stanley Industrial Alliance Stage (a moniker that not a single Vancouverite uses), the Stanley is part of the Arts Club Theatre Company, Vancouver's biggest. (📞604-687-1644; www.artsclub.com; 2750 Granville St, South Granville; tickets from $29; ⏱Sep-Jul; 🚌10)

Kino

CABARET

15 ⭐ MAP P120, E4

Vancouver's only flamenco cafe is a great place to chill on a summer evening. If it's really warm, bask in the sun with a beer outside. But be sure to trip back in when the show starts: there's live dancing on the little wooden side stage from Wednesday to Saturday, with jazz, bluegrass and comedy also popping up regularly on other nights. (📞604-875-1998; www.thekino.ca; 3456 Cambie St, Cambie Village; tickets from $5; ⏱5pm-1am Mon-Fri, 3pm-1am Sat, 3pm-midnight Sun; 🚌15)

Vancouver Canadians

BASEBALL

16 ⭐ MAP P120, F7

Minor-league affiliates of the Toronto Blue Jays, the Canadians play at the charmingly old-school

Summertime Ballgames

Catching a **Vancouver Canadians** minor league baseball game at old-school **Nat Bailey Stadium** is a summer tradition for many locals. But for some, the experience isn't complete unless you also add a hot dog and some ice-cold beers to the proceedings. Enhancing the festivities are the nonbaseball shenanigans, ranging from kiss cams to mascot races. Arguably the most fun you can have at a Vancouver spectator sport, it's also one of the most budget-friendly options (depending on how many hot dogs you put away).

Nat Bailey Stadium. It's known as 'the prettiest ballpark in the world' thanks to its mountain backdrop. Afternoon games – called 'nooners' – are perfect for a nostalgic bask in the sun. Hot dogs and beer rule the menu, but there's also sushi and fruit – this is Vancouver, after all. (☎604-872-5232; www.milb.com/vancouver; 4601 Ontario St, Nat Bailey Stadium; tickets from $15; ☉Jun-Aug; ♦♦; ☐33, Ⓢ King Edward)

Shopping

Pacific Arts Market   ARTS & CRAFTS

17 🅐 MAP P120, B2

Head upstairs to this large, under-the-radar gallery space and you'll find a kaleidoscopic array of stands showcasing the work of 40+ Vancouver and BC artists. From paintings to jewelry and from fiber arts to handmade chocolate bars, it's the perfect spot to find authentic souvenirs to take back home. The artists change regularly and there's something for every budget here. (☎778-877-6449; www.pacificartsmarket.ca; 1448 W Broadway, South Granville; ☉noon-5:30pm Tue & Wed, noon-7pm Thu & Fri, 11am-7pm Sat, 1-5pm Sun; ☐9)

Walrus   HOME WARES

18 🅐 MAP P120, E4

A small but brilliantly curated store teeming with must-have accessories and home wares, mostly from Canadian designers. Form meets function with everything on the shelves here, so give yourself plenty of time to browse the perfect pottery knickknacks, quirky artisan jewelry and raft of irresistible bags from Vancouver favorite Herschel Supply Co. (☎604-874-9770; www.walrushome.com; 3408 Cambie St, Cambie Village; ☉10am-6pm Mon-Fri, 10am-5pm Sat, noon-5pm Sun; ☐15)

Bacci's

HOME WARES, CLOTHING

19 🔒 MAP P120, A3

Combining designer women's clothing on one side with a room full of perfectly curated trinkets piled high on antique wooden tables on the other, Bacci's is a dangerous place to browse. Before you know it, you'll have an armful of chunky luxury soaps, embroidered cushions and picture-perfect coffee mugs to fit in your suitcase. (📞604-733-4933; www.baccis.ca; 2788 Granville St, South Granville; 🕑9:45am-5:45pm Mon-Sat; 🚌10)

Purdy's Chocolates

CHOCOLATE

20 🔒 MAP P120, A3

Like a sweet beacon to the weary, this purple-painted chocolate purveyor stands at the corner of Granville and W 11th Ave calling your name. It's a homegrown BC business with outlets dotted like candy sprinkles across the city, and it's hard not to pick up a few treats: go for chocolate hedgehogs, orange meltie bars or sweet Georgia browns – pecans in caramel and chocolate. (📞604-732-7003; www.purdys.com; 2705 Granville St, South Granville; 🕑10am-6pm Mon-Sat, noon-5pm Sun; 🚌10)

Meinhardt Fine Foods

FOOD

21 🔒 MAP P120, A3

The culinary equivalent of a sex shop for food fans, this swanky deli and grocery emporium's narrow aisles are lined with international condiments, luxury canned goods and the kind of alluring treats that everyone should try at least once. Build a perfect picnic from the tempting bread, cheese and cold cuts, or snag one of the house-made deli sandwiches (paprika chicken recommended). (📞604-732-4405; www.meinhardt.com; 3002 Granville St, South Granville; 🕑7am-9pm Mon-Sat, 9am-8pm Sun; 🚌10)

Explore ◈
Kitsilano & University of British Columbia

Occupying the forest-fringed peninsula south of downtown, Vancouver's West Side includes two highlight neighborhoods: Kitsilano, with its large beaches, wood-built heritage homes and browsable 4th Ave shopping and dining district; plus the University of British Columbia (UBC), a verdant campus with enough museums, attractions and dining options for a great alternative day out from the city center.

The Short List

○ **Museum of Anthropology (p132)** Exploring Vancouver's best museum, with its spectacular Aboriginal artifacts and exhibits from around the world.

○ **Museum of Vancouver (p138)** Noodling around nostalgic displays that illuminate the yesteryear city.

○ **Kitsilano Beach (p138)** Sunning yourself on the area's best beach before catching a free Kitsilano Showboat performance.

Getting There & Around

🚌 Services 4 and 9 run through Kitsilano to UBC. The 99B-Line express bus runs along Broadway to UBC.

🚌 Take a Canada Line SkyTrain from downtown to Broadway-City Hall, then board the 99B-Line to UBC.

🚗 There is metered parking on and around W 4th and Broadway in Kitsilano. UBC has parkades and metered parking.

Kitsilano & University of BC Map on p136

Kitsilano Beach (p138) IRRA / SHUTTERSTOCK©

Top Experience 📸

See the Forest of Totem Poles at the Museum of Anthropology

👁 MAP P136, A3

Vancouver's best museum is the main reason many visitors come to the University of British Columbia campus. The MOA is home to one of Canada's finest and most important collections of Northwest Coast Aboriginal art and artifacts. But the ambitious collection here goes way beyond local anthropological treasures, illuminating diverse cultures from around the world.

www.moa.ubc.ca

6393 NW Marine Dr, UBC

adult/child $18/16

🕙 10am-5pm Fri-Wed, 10am-9pm Thu, closed Mon Oct-May

🚌 99B-Line, then 68

MOA 101

The highlight of the Arthur Erickson–designed museum, the **Great Hall** is a forest of towering totem poles plus a menagerie of carved ceremonial figures, house posts and delicate exhibits – all set against a giant floor-to-ceiling window facing the waterfront and mountains. Many carvings are surprisingly vibrantly colored: look out for smiling masks plus a life-size rowing boat containing two figures that look ready to head straight out to sea. The Great Hall is also where the museum's **free tours** start several times a day: these are highly recommended since they provide an excellent overview of what else there is to see here.

Getting Lost

This is also a great museum to lose yourself in. The **Gallery of Northwest Coast Masterworks** combines breathtaking smaller creations, such as intricate ceremonial headdresses, with the recorded voices of Aboriginal artisans contextualizing the exhibits. Nearby, the jam-packed **Multiversity Galleries** teem with 10,000 ethnographic artifacts from around the world, with everything from Kenyan snuff bottles to Swedish lace doilies. Save time for the **European Ceramics Gallery**, a subtle stunner lined with pottery and porcelain made between the 16th and 19th centuries.

Value-Added Extras

There are also some diverse temporary exhibitions staged here throughout the year. Shows have ranged from Nairobi photography to puppets from around the world. Check MOA's website for upcoming openings. And, if it's a fine day, discover the site's **Outdoor Exhibits** area, with its Haida houses and Musqueam house posts.

★ **Top Tips**

o Admission is cut to $10 from 5pm to 9pm every Thursday.

o There are free tours, included with entry, on most days. Check at the front desk for times.

o Entry to the Outdoor Exhibits area is free and does not require a ticket.

o There are several other attractions on campus; ask at the front desk for combined ticket options that include entry to some of these other UBC sites.

✕ **Take a Break**

The MOA is a short walk from the excellent Koerner's Pub (p143), where you can drink and dine with the students.

Time your visit well and you can also pick up a few treats at one of the **UBC Farm Markets** (☏604-822-5092; www.ubcfarm.ubc.ca/farm-markets; 3461 Ross Dr, UBC; ◷10am-2pm Sat Jun-Nov; ♿; ▯99B-Line).

Walking Tour 🥾

UBC Campus & Gardens Walk

The region's biggest university campus has plenty of attractions for a full day out. But while transit makes it easy to reach from downtown, you'll feel like you've traveled far from the city. This walk leads you to some of UBC's biggest and also lesser-known attractions. Keep your eyes peeled en route for the many public artworks that dot the campus.

Walk Facts

Start Museum of Anthropology

End UBC Botanical Garden

Length 3km; 1½ hours

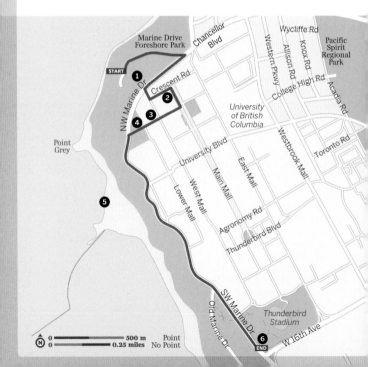

❶ Museum of Anthropology

Vancouver's best museum (MOA; p132) illuminates the rich culture and artistry of the region's original residents. But there's also a sided-ish of eye-popping ethnographic artifacts from around the world to plunge into here. Give yourself plenty of time to explore and take a free guided tour if you have time.

❷ Morris & Helen Belkin Art Gallery

One of Vancouver's oldest contemporary art spaces, the Morris & Helen Belkin Art Gallery (p140) stages changing (and sometimes quite challenging) exhibitions that are always worth checking out. Check ahead for openings.

❸ UBC Asian Centre

The campus is studded with landscaped gardens and green spaces but the one outside the UBC Asian Centre is arguably the most unusual. Check out the hulking rock garden boulders here, each inscribed with Confucian philosophies.

❹ Nitobe Memorial Garden

Just a few steps away, the utterly delightful Nitobe Memorial Garden (p139) is an oasis of traditional Japanese horticultural tranquility. Look for turtles basking in the pond's grass-banked shoreline and check ahead for summertime tours that explain some of the garden's symbolic features.

❺ Wreck Beach

If you're feeling adventurous, look for the signs for Trail 6, walk between the trees and descend to Wreck Beach. Vancouver's official naturist beach, it's the perfect opportunity to drop your drawers with a few like-minded locals.

❻ UBC Botanical Garden

Make sure you put your pants back on before reaching your final attraction. UBC Botanical Garden (p138) is a verdant green space that's divided into a dense forest swathe on one side and several themed horticultural areas on the other. Take a canopy walkway tour (p140) while you're here.

Don't Miss the Shop

While many museum stores are lame afterthoughts offering cheesy trinkets, MOA's version is far superior, including authentic Aboriginal arts and crafts created by local artisans. Look for unique carved masks plus intricately engraved gold and silver jewelry here. In fact, you could start your own anthropology museum when you get back home.

Ⓝ N

0 ———————————— 1 km
0 ———————————— 0.5 miles

Burrard
Inlet

Spanish Banks
Beach Park

NW Marine Dr

Marine Drive
Foreshore
Park

Acadia Rd

Kingston Rd

Pacific Spirit
Regional Park

Chancellor Blvd

Bianca St

Tolmie St

Belmont Ave

W 2nd Ave

**Museum of
Anthropology**

NW Marine Dr

Knox Rd

Allison Rd

Western Pkwy

W 3rd Ave

W 4th Ave

Ⓜ 7 Morris &
Helen Belkin
Art Gallery

13

University Blvd

W 6th Ave

West Point
Grey Park

W 8th Ave

Ⓜ 5

Main Mall

9

University
of British
Columbia

W 10th Ave

Nitobe
Memorial
Garden

3
Beaty
Biodiversity
Museum

Westbrook Mall

W 12th Ave

W 14th Ave

Sasamat St

Trimble St

Discovery St

University
Golf Club

W 16th Ave

East Mall

UBC
Botanical
Garden

West Mall

Thunderbird
Stadium

W 16th Ave

Old Marine Dr

4

6 Greenheart
TreeWalk

Pacific Spirit
Regional Park

Point
No Point

SW Marine Dr

Imperial Rd

DUNBAR

Strait of
Georgia

Marine Drive
Foreshore Park

SW Marine Dr

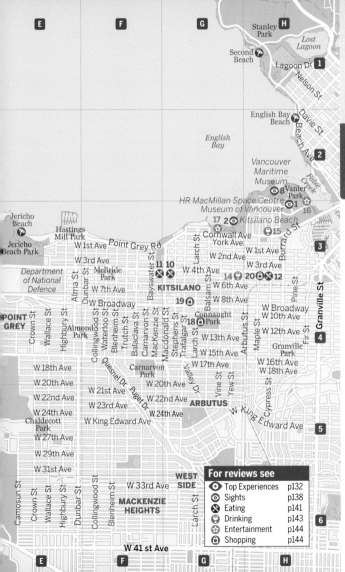

Kitsilano & University of British Columbia

E

F

G

H

Stanley Park

Lost Lagoon

Second Beach

Lagoon Dr

Nelson St

1

English Bay Beach

Davie St

Beach Ave

English Bay

2

Vancouver Maritime Museum

False Creek

HR MacMillan Space Centre
Museum of Vancouver

8 Vanier Park
1
16

17 2 Kitsilano Beach

Jericho Beach

Hastings Mill Park

Point Grey Rd

Cornwall Ave
York Ave

15

Burrard St

Jericho Beach Park

W 1st Ave

W 1st Ave

3

W 3rd Ave

Department of National Defence

McBride Park

W 3rd Ave

Alma St

Dunbar St

Bayswater St

11 10

W 4th Ave

Larch St

W 2nd Ave
W 3rd Ave

Pine St

W 7th Ave

KITSILANO

14 20 12

W 6th Ave

Balsam St

Granville St

4

POINT GREY

W Broadway

19

W 8th Ave

W Broadway

Fir St

Crown St

Wallace St

Highbury St

Almond Park

Collingwood St

Waterloo St

Blenheim St

Trutch St

Balaclava St

Carnarvon St

Mackenzie St

Macdonald St

Stephens St

Trafalgar St

Larch St

Connaught Park

18

Arbutus St

Maple St

W 10th Ave

W 12th Ave

Granville Park

W 13th Ave

W 15th Ave

W 16th Ave

W 18th Ave

Quesnel Dr

Carnarvon Park

W 17th Ave

Valley Dr

Vine St

Yew St

Cypress St

W 18th Ave

W 20th Ave

W 21st Ave

Puget Dr

W 20th Ave

W 22nd Ave

ARBUTUS

5

W 22nd Ave

W 23rd Ave

W 24th Ave

W King Edward Ave

Chaldecott Park

W 24th Ave

W King Edward Ave

W 27th Ave

W 29th Ave

W 31st Ave

Camosun St

Crown St

Wallace St

Highbury St

Dunbar St

Collingwood St

Blenheim St

W 33rd Ave

WEST SIDE

Larch St

MACKENZIE HEIGHTS

6

W 41st Ave

E

F

G

H

For reviews see	
⦿ Top Experiences	p132
◉ Sights	p138
✖ Eating	p141
◗ Drinking	p143
✿ Entertainment	p144
🔒 Shopping	p144

Sights

Museum of Vancouver MUSEUM

1 ◎ MAP P136, H3

The MOV serves up cool temporary exhibitions alongside in-depth permanent galleries of fascinating First Nations artifacts and evocative pioneer-era exhibits. But it really comes to life in its vibrant 1950s pop culture and 1960s hippie counterculture sections, a reminder that Kitsilano was once the grass-smoking centre of Vancouver's flower-power movement. Don't miss the shimmering gallery of vintage neon signs collected from around the city; it's a favorite with locals. (MOV; ☎604-736-4431; www. museumofvancouver.ca; 1100 Chestnut St, Kitsilano; adult/child $20.50/9.75; ⊙10am-5pm Sun-Wed, to 8pm Thu, to 9pm Fri & Sat; ℗⍾; ➌2)

Kitsilano Beach BEACH

2 ◎ MAP P136, G3

Facing English Bay, Kits Beach is one of Vancouver's favorite summertime hangouts. The wide, sandy expanse attracts Frisbee tossers and volleyball players, and those who just like to preen while catching the rays. The ocean is fine for a dip, though serious swimmers should consider the heated **Kitsilano Pool** (www.vancouverparks.ca; 2305 Cornwall Ave, Kitsilano; adult/child $6.10/3.05; ⊙7am-evening mid-Jun–Sep; ➌2), one of the world's largest outdoor saltwater pools. (cnr Cornwall Ave & Arbutus St, Kitsilano; ➌2)

Beaty Biodiversity Museum MUSEUM

3 ◎ MAP P136, A4

A family friendly museum showcasing a two-million-item natural history collection including birds, fossils and herbarium displays. The highlight is the 25m blue-whale skeleton, artfully displayed in the two-story entranceway. Don't miss the first display case, which is crammed with a beady-eyed menagerie of tooth-and-claw taxidermy. Consider visiting on the third Thursday of the month when entry is by donation after 5pm and the museum stays open until 8:30pm; there's often a special theme or live performance for these monthly nocturnal events. (☎604-827-4955; www.beatymuseum .ubc.ca; 2212 Main Mall, UBC; adult/child $14/10; ⊙10am-5pm Tue-Sun; ⍾; ➌99B-Line)

UBC Botanical Garden GARDENS

4 ◎ MAP P136, A5

You'll find a huge array of rhododendrons, a fascinating apothecary plot and a winter green space of off-season bloomers in this 28-hectare complex of themed gardens. Among the towering trees, look for northern flicker woodpeckers and chittering little Douglas squirrels, but save time for the attraction's April-to-October Greenheart TreeWalk (p140), which elevates visitors up to 23m above the forest floor on a 310m guided ecotour. Combined garden and Greenheart tickets cost adult/child $23/10. (☎604-822-4208; www.botanicalgarden.ubc.ca; 6804 SW Marine Dr, UBC; adult/child $10/5; ⏰10am-4:30pm; ♿; 🚌99B-Line, then 68)

Nitobe Memorial Garden
GARDENS

5 ◉ MAP P136, A3

Exemplifying Japanese horticultural philosophies, this is a delightfully tranquil green oasis of peaceful pathways, small traditional bridges and a large, moss-banked pond filled with plump koi carp. It's named after Dr Inazo Nitobe, a scholar whose mug appears on Japan's ¥5000 bill. Consider a springtime visit for the florid cherry blossom displays and keep an eye out for the occasional turtle basking in the sun. (☎604-822-6038; www.botanicalgarden.ubc.ca/nitobe; 1895 Lower Mall, UBC; adult/child $7/4 Apr-Oct, by donation Nov-Mar; ⏰10am-4:30pm Apr-Oct, 10am-2pm Mon-Fri Nov-Mar; 🚌99B-Line, then 68)

HR MacMillan Space Centre
MUSEUM

Focusing on the wonderful world of space, admission to this kid-favorite museum at the Museum of Vancouver (see 1 ◉ Map p136, H3) includes a gallery of hands-on exhibits (don't miss the Mars section where you can drive across the surface in a simulator) as well as a menu of live science demonstrations in the small theater and a cool 45-minute planetarium show

Kitsilano Pool

Save Your Dosh in Vancouver

The **Vanier Park Explore Pass** costs adult/child $42.50/36.40 and covers entry to the Museum of Vancouver (MOV), Vancouver Maritime Museum and HR MacMillan Space Centre. It's available at each of the three attractions and can save you around $10 on individual adult entry. There is also an alternative **Dual Pass** (adult/child $31.50/18.50) that covers the MOV and the Space Centre only.

You can also save with two separate passes at the university. The **UBC Museums Pass** (adult/child/family $25/20/60) includes entry to the Museum of Anthropology (MOA) and Beaty Biodiversity Museum, while the **UBC Gardens and MOA Pass** (adult/child/family $27/23/65) covers the Museum of Anthropology, UBC Botanical Garden and Nitobe Memorial Garden.

upstairs. Check the daily schedule of shows and presentations online before you arrive. The Saturday-night planetarium performances are popular with locals and typically draw a more adult crowd. (📞604-738-7827; www.spacecentre.ca; 1100 Chestnut St, Kitsilano; adult/child $19.50/14; ⏲10am-5pm Jul & Aug, reduced hours off-season; 🅿🚻; 🚌2)

Greenheart TreeWalk
WALK

6 ◉ MAP P136, B5

One of the best ways to commune with nature is to pretend you're a squirrel. While costumes are not required for this cool canopy walkway (you may win a raised eyebrow if you chance it), visitors love swaying across the steel bridges and noodling around the wooden platforms up to 23m from the forest floor. Located inside UBC Botanical Garden (p138), Greenheart admission includes entry to that attraction. (📞604-822-4208; www.botanicalgarden.ubc.ca; 6804 SW Marine Dr, UBC Botanical Garden, UBC; adult/child $23/10; ⏲Apr-Oct; 🅿🚻; 🚌99B-Line, then 68)

Morris & Helen Belkin Art Gallery
GALLERY

7 ◉ MAP P136, A3

This ever-intriguing gallery specializes in contemporary and often quite challenging pieces, with chin-stroking new exhibitions opening in its high-ceilinged, white-walled spaces throughout the year. Check ahead for workshops and presentations, often covering key or emerging themes in avant-garde art. (📞604-822-2759; www.belkin.ubc.ca; 1825 Main Mall, UBC; admission free; ⏲10am-5pm Tue-Fri, noon-5pm Sat & Sun; 🚌99B-Line, then 68)

Vancouver Maritime Museum

MUSEUM

8 ⦿ MAP P136, H2

Teeming with salty seafaring artifacts, dozens of intricate ship models and a couple of walk-through recreated boat sections, the prize exhibit at this waterfront A-frame museum is the *St Roch*, a 1928 Royal Canadian Mounted Police Arctic patrol vessel that was the first to navigate the Northwest Passage in both directions. Entry includes timed access to this celebrated boat and you can also try your hand at piloting it via a cool wheelhouse simulator. (📞604-257-8300; www.vancouvermaritime museum.com; 1905 Ogden Ave, Kitsilano; adult/child $13.50/10; ⏱10am-5pm Fri-Wed, to 8pm Thu; P 🚻; 🚌2)

Eating

Jamjar Canteen

LEBANESE $

9 ❌ MAP P136, A3

Visiting Canteen, a simplified version of the city's highly popular Jamjar Lebanese comfort food restaurants, means choosing from four mains (lamb sausages or deep-fried cauliflower recommended) then adding the approach: rice bowl, salad bowl or wrap. Choices of olives, veggies, hummus and more are then requested before you can dive into your hearty lunch or dinner. (📞604-620-5320; www. jamjarcanteen.ca; 6035 University Blvd, UBC; mains $10-12; ⏱10:30am-10pm Mon-Fri, to 9pm Sat & Sun; 🛜🖊; 🚌99B-Line)

Naam

VEGETARIAN $

10 ❌ MAP P136, G3

An evocative relic of Kitsilano's hippie past, this vegetarian restaurant has the feel of a comfy farmhouse. It's not unusual to wait for a table at peak times, but it's worth it for the huge menu of hearty stir-fries, nightly curry specials, bulging quesadillas and ever-popular fries with miso gravy. It's the kind of veggie spot where carnivores delightedly dine. (📞604-738-7151; www.thenaam.com; 2724 W 4th Ave, Kitsilano; mains $9-17; ⏱24hr; 🖊; 🚌4)

Linh Cafe

FRENCH, VIETNAMESE $$

11 ❌ MAP P136, F3

Arrive off-peak (limited reservations are also available) at this chatty locals' favorite, a friendly, red-tabled restaurant serving French bistro classics and enticing Vietnamese specialties. You'll find everything from escargot to steak frites on the eclectic menu, but we recommend the deliciously brothy beef pho. On your way out, add a shiny little palmier pastry and a Vietnamese coffee to go. (📞604-559-4668; www.linhcafe.com; 2836 W 4th Ave, Kitsilano; mains $14-45; ⏱11am-9pm Wed-Fri, 10am-9pm Sat & Sun; 🛜; 🚌4)

The Dope on Local Pot Shops

Backstory

Just a few years ago, Vancouver had dozens of storefront marijuana dispensaries operating in a gray area of law that accepted the personal use of cannabis for medical reasons. Many locals and several of these stores made an art form out of proving this medical need.

Law Change

This pot smoke of confusion cleared in 2018 when the federal government legalized the recreational use of cannabis in Canada. Quickly, the city and the province moved to regulate this 'Wild West' industry here. Rather than navigate through the rigorous licensing laws that ensued, many weed stores that had popped up over the last few years suddenly shut down.

Pot Shops Go Legit

The 2.0 version of Vancouver's cannabis retail scene is now emerging, with licensed shops and chains including City Cannabis Co, Hobo Recreational Cannabis and Evergreen Cannabis Society. The province's BC Liquor Distribution Branch, longtime controller of booze sales in the region, is now the only legal way for private pot shops to source supplies for recreational resale. It remains to be seen if this business model will thrive, or if longtime 'BC bud' users will keep buying from their friendly neighborhood suppliers.

Need to Know

If you're curious about these stores, nip inside and chat to the staff about how it all works and what they can sell you. Keep in mind that although recreational cannabis is now legal in Canada, you are not permitted to transport your purchases across international borders. For more informtion read up via the province's BC Cannabis Stores website at www.bccannabisstores.com.

Fable Kitchen

CANADIAN $$

12 MAP P136, H3

One of Vancouver's favorite farm-to-table restaurants is a lovely rustic-chic room of exposed brick, wood beams and prominently displayed red rooster logos. But looks are just part of the appeal. Expect perfectly prepared bistro dishes showcasing local seasonal ingredients such as duck, pork and scallops. It's great gourmet comfort food with little pretension, hence the packed room most nights. Reservations recommended.

(📞604-732-1322; www.fablekitchen.ca; 1944 W 4th Ave, Kitsilano; mains $21-28; 🕐11am-2:30pm & 5:30-10pm Tue-Fri, 10am-2pm & 5-10pm Sat & Sun; 🚌4)

Drinking

Koerner's Pub
PUB

13 🚇 MAP P136, A3

UBC's best pub welcomes with its communal tables, foliage-fringed patio and clientele of nerdy professors and hipster regulars. There's an excellent booze list; dive into BC craft beers from the likes of Driftwood and Strange Fellows. Food-wise, the Koerner Organic Burger is a staple, but also try the crunchy UBC Farm Harvest Salad, largely sourced from the university's own farm.

(📞604-827-1443; www.koerners.ca; 6371 Crescent Rd, UBC; 🕐11:30am-10:30pm Mon & Tue, to midnight Wed-Fri; 🚌99B-Line)

49th Parallel Coffee
COFFEE

14 🚇 MAP P136, G3

Kitsilano's favorite coffee shop hangout. Sit with the locals in the glass-enclosed conservatory-like area (handy in deluge-prone Raincouver) while sipping your latte in a turquoise cup and scoffing as many own-brand Luckys Doughnuts as you can manage; just because they're artisanal, doesn't mean you should have only one. Need a recommendation? Try an apple-bacon fritter. Or two. (📞604-420-

49th Parallel Coffee

4901; www.49thcafe.com; 2198 W 4th Ave, Kitsilano; ⏱7am-7pm Sun-Thu, to 8pm Fri & Sat; 🛜; 🚌4)

Corduroy   BAR

15 🚇 MAP P136, H3

Near the first bus stop after the Burrard Bridge (coming from downtown), this intimate, cave-like hangout is arguably Kitsilano's best late-night haunt. Slide onto a seat and peruse the beady-eyed taxidermy, then order a pitcher of house beer from the shingle-backed bar. A lively show roster (check ahead via its Facebook page) often includes bands, comedy or open-mike shenanigans. (📞604-733-0162; www.corduroyrestaurant.com; 1943 Cornwall Ave, Kitsilano; ⏱4pm-2am Mon-Sat, to midnight Sun; 🛜; 🚌2)

Entertainment

Bard on the Beach   PERFORMING ARTS

16 ⭐ MAP P136, H3

Watching Shakespeare performed while the sun sets over the mountains beyond the tented main stage is a Vancouver summertime highlight. There are usually three Shakespeare plays, plus one Bard-related work (*Rosencrantz and Guildenstern are Dead,* for example), to choose from during the season. Q&A talks are staged after some Tuesday performances; also opera, fireworks and wine-tasting special nights throughout the season. (📞604-739-0559; www.

bardonthebeach.org; 1695 Whyte Ave, Vanier Park, Kitsilano; tickets from $24; ⏱Jun-Sep; ♿; 🚌2)

Kitsilano Showboat   CONCERT VENUE

17 ⭐ MAP P136, G3

An 80-year-old tradition that generations of locals know and love, this alfresco waterfront stage near Kits Pool offers free shows and concerts in summer. Grab a bleacher-style seat facing the North Shore mountains and prepare for singers, musicians, dancers and more; check the online schedule to see what's coming up. A great way to mingle with the chatty locals. (📞604-734-7332; www.kitsilanoshowboat.com; 2300 Cornwall Ave, Kitsilano; free; ⏱7pm Mon, Wed, Fri & Sat Jun-Aug; ♿; 🚌2)

Shopping

Kitsilano Farmers Market   MARKET

18 🅿 MAP P136, G4

Kitsilano's best excuse to get out and hang with the locals, this seasonal farmers market is one of the city's most popular. Arrive early for the best selection and you'll have the pick of freshly plucked local fruit and veg, such as sweet strawberries or spectacularly flavorful heirloom tomatoes. You'll likely never want to shop in a mainstream supermarket again. (www.eatlocal.org; 2690 Larch St, Kitsilano Community Centre, Kitsilano; ⏱10am-2pm Sun May-Oct; 🚌9)

Vancouver's Bold New Park

When the City of Vancouver splashed out $55 million on an 8.5km stretch of disused railway line running from Kitsilano to Marpole, some locals questioned the purchase. The **Arbutus Greenway** has since become popular with locals who love walking or cycling this wide, nature-hugging trail. Plans are still being finalized for the park's permanent features but whatever happens this flora-flanked corridor is here to stay.

Kidsbooks

BOOKS

19 MAP P136, G4

From *Dolphin Boy* to *The Wonky Donkey*, this huge, highly inviting store – reputedly Canada's biggest children's bookshop – has thousands of novels, picture books and anything else you can think of to keep your bookish sprogs happy. There are regular author events (check details ahead via the website) plus quality toys and games to provide a break from all that strenuous page-turning. (604-738-5335; www.kidsbooks.ca; 2557 W Broadway, Kitsilano; 9:30am-6pm Mon-Thu & Sat, 9:30am-9pm Fri, 11am-6pm Sun; 9)

Zulu Records

MUSIC

20 MAP P136, H3

Kitsilano's fave indie music store has downsized in recent years, but it's still easy to blow an afternoon here with the vinyl and CD nerds, flicking through the new and used and hard-to-find albums. It also sells local show tickets, while the knowledgeable staffers can point you to essential Vancouver recordings worth buying. (604-738-3232; www. zulurecords.com; 1972 W 4th Ave, Kitsilano; 10:30am-7pm Mon-Wed, 10:30am-9pm Thu & Fri, 9:30am-6:30pm Sat, noon-6pm Sun; 4)

Survival Guide

Before You Go

Book Your Stay

o More than 23,000 hotel, B&B and hostel rooms, the majority in or around downtown.

o Book far ahead for summer. Rates peak in July and August, but there are good spring and fall deals.

o Airbnb operates in Vancouver, although a regulatory crackdown has reduced numbers.

Useful Websites

Tourism Vancouver (www.tourismvancouver.com) Wide range of listings and package deals.

Hello BC (www.hellobc.com) Official Destination British Columbia (BC) accommodations search engine.

Accredited BC Accommodations Association (www.accrediteddaccommodations.ca) Wide range of B&Bs in Vancouver and around the province.

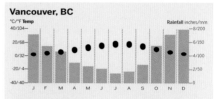

Vancouver, BC

When to Go

o **Winter (Dec-Feb)** Chilly and damp but rarely snowy, except on local ski slopes. Some clear but crisp days included.

o **Spring (Mar-May)** Rain, some sun and good off-peak hotel rates.

o **Summer (Jun-Aug)** Vancouver's blue-skied peak. Expect crowded visitor attractions.

o **Fall (Sep-Oct)** Rain returns but still plenty of golden sunny days as the leaves descend. Another good time for hotel deals.

Lonely Planet (www.lonelyplanet.com/canada/vancouver/hotels) Recommendations.

Best Budget

YWCA Hotel (www.ywcahotel.com) Centrally located with comfortable rooms that offer great value (especially for families).

HI Vancouver Downtown (www.hihostels.ca) Actually located in the West End; a quieter hostel with good family rooms.

Samesun Backpackers Lodge (www.

samesun.com) Right on downtown's Granville Strip entertainment district; perfect for partyers.

Best Midrange

Victorian Hotel (www.victorianhotel.ca) Excellent downtown location; mix of large and pension-style smaller rooms.

Sunset Inn & Suites (www.sunsetinn.com) West End hotel with large, kitchen-equipped rooms.

Sylvia Hotel (www.sylviahotel.com)

Ivy-covered heritage hotel with some waterfront view rooms.

Best Top End

Fairmont Pacific Rim (www.fairmont. com) Chic downtown property steps from the waterfront.

St Regis Hotel (www. stregishotel.com) City-center accommodations with some excellent amenities.

Rosewood Hotel Georgia (www.rose woodhotels.com) Stylish sleepover for those who like to see and be seen.

Arriving in Vancouver

Vancouver International Airport

○ Located 13km south of Vancouver in the city of Richmond, **YVR** (YVR; 604-207-7077; www.yvr. ca; 3211 Grant McConachie Way, Richmond;) has two main terminals and receives flights from BC, North America and around the world.

○ Canada Line SkyTrain runs from the airport to Vancouver, taking 25 minutes to reach downtown and costing from $8.05 to $10.90.

○ Taxi fares to downtown are around $35.

○ Hire car desks are located inside the airport.

Pacific Central Station

○ **Pacific Central Station** (1150 Station St, Chinatown; S Main St-Science World) is the city's main terminus for long-distance trains from across Canada on VIA Rail (www.viarail.com), and from Seattle (just south of the border) and beyond on Amtrak (www.amtrak.com).

○ Intercity bus services also roll in here including **Greyhound** (www. greyhound.com) services from Seattle, **BC Connector** (www. bcconnector.com) services from Kelowna, Kamloops, Whistler and Victoria.

○ The Main St-Science World SkyTrain station is just across the street for connections to downtown and beyond.

○ There are car-rental

desks in the station and cabs are also available just outside the building.

BC Ferries

○ **BC Ferries** (250-386-3431; www.bcferries.com) arrive at Tsawwassen, an hour south of Vancouver, and at Horseshoe Bay, 30 minutes from downtown in West Vancouver. These services arrive from points around British Columbia, including, Victoria.

○ To reach downtown from Tsawwassen via transit, take bus 620 (adult/child $5.90/4.05) to Bridgeport Station in Richmond and transfer to the Canada Line. It takes about an hour to reach the city center.

○ From Horseshoe Bay to downtown, take bus 257 (adult/child $4.35/3). It takes about 40 minutes.

Getting Around

Bus

○ Vancouver's **TransLink** (www.translink.ca) bus network is extensive. All vehicles are equipped with bike racks and all are wheelchair accessible.

○ Exact change (or more) is required; buses use fare machines and change is not given. Tickets are valid for up to 90 minutes of transfer travel. While Vancouver's transit system covers three geographic fare zones, all bus trips are regarded as one-zone fares.

○ Bus services operate from early morning to after midnight in central areas. There is also an additional 12-route NightBus system that runs from 2am. Look for NightBus signs at designated stops.

SkyTrain

○ TransLink's SkyTrain rapid-transit network is a great way to move around the region, especially beyond the city center.

○ Compass tickets for SkyTrain trips can be purchased from station vending machines (change is given; machines also accept debit and credit cards) prior to boarding.

○ SkyTrain's Canada Line links the city to Richmond and the airport.

○ The Expo Line operates services from downtown to the cities of Surrey and Burnaby.

○ The Millennium Line links Vancouver's VCC-Clark Station to the cities of Burnaby, Coquitlam and Port Moody.

SeaBus

○ The iconic SeaBus public transit water shuttle (regular transit fares apply) takes 15 minutes to cross Burrard Inlet between Waterfront Station and North Vancouver's Lonsdale Quay.

○ At Lonsdale you can then connect to buses servicing North Vancouver and West Vancouver; including the 236 to both Capilano Suspension Bridge and Grouse Mountain.

○ SeaBus services leave from Waterfront Station between 6:16am and 1:22am, Monday to Saturday (8:16am to 11:16pm on Sunday).

○ Tickets must be purchased from vending machines on either side of the route before boarding.

Miniferry

○ There are two private miniferry operators in the city. Single trips on either operator cost from $3.50.

○ **Aquabus Ferries** (☎604-689-5858; www. theaquabus.com) runs between the foot of Hornby St and Granville Island. It also services several additional spots along the False Creek waterfront, as far as Science World.

○ **False Creek Ferries** (☎604-684-7781; www. granvilleislandferries.bc.ca) operates a similar Granville Island service from Sunset Beach, and has additional ports of call around False Creek.

Bicycle

○ Vancouver is a good cycling city, with 300km of designated routes.

○ You can take your bike for free on SkyTrain, SeaBus and regular bus transit services. Cyclists are required by law to wear helmets.

○ Locals and visitors can use **Mobi** (☎778-655-1800; www.mobibikes. ca), a public bike-share scheme.

○ Download free cycle route maps

Transit Tickets & Passes

○ Along with trip-planning resources, the TransLink website (www.translink.ca) has a comprehensive section on fares and passes covering its combined bus, SeaBus and SkyTrain services.

○ The transit system is divided into three geographic zones. One-zone trips cost adult/child $3/1.95, two-zones $4.25/2.95 and three-zones $5.75/3.95. All bus trips are one-zone fares. If you buy a stored value plastic Compass Card, fares are charged at a lower rate.

○ You can buy single-use paper tickets and all-access paper DayPasses (adult/child $10.50/8.25) from vending machines at SeaBus and SkyTrain stations. You can also buy stored value Compass Cards ($6 deposit) from these machines or at designated Compass retailers around the city, including London Drugs branches.

○ After 6:30pm, and on weekends or holidays, all transit trips are classed as one-zone fares. Children under five travel for free on all transit services at all times.

from the TransLink website (www.translink.ca) or plan your route using https://vancouver.bikerouteplanner.com.

Car & Motorcycle

○ For most Vancouver sightseeing, you'll be fine without a car.

○ For visits to the wider region's mountains and communities, a vehicle makes life much simpler.

○ Parking is at a premium in downtown Vancouver: there are some free spots on residential side streets but many require permits, and traffic wardens are predictably predatory. For an interactive map of parking-lot locations, check EasyPark (www.easypark.ca).

Taxi

At time of research, Vancouver was in the process of paving the way for ride-hailing schemes such as Uber and Lyft. Until then, try these taxi companies:

Black Top & Checker Cabs (📞 604-731-1111; www.btccabs.ca; 🚕)

Vancouver Taxi (📞 604-871-1111; www.vancouvertaxi.cab)

Yellow Cab (📞 604-681-1111; www.yellowcabonline.com; 🚕)

Essential Information

Accessible Travel

○ On your arrival at the airport, vehicle-rental agencies can provide prearranged cars with hand controls. Accessible cabs are widely available at the airport and throughout the city, on request.

○ All TransLink SkyTrain, SeaBus and transit bus services are wheelchair accessible. Check the TransLink website (www.translink.ca) for information on accessible transport around the region. Head to www.accesstotravel.gc.ca for information and resources on accessible travel across Canada. In addition, download Lonely Planet's free Accessible Travel guides from http://lptravel.to/AccessibleTravel.

o Service dogs may legally be brought into restaurants, hotels and other businesses.

o Almost all downtown sidewalks have ramps, and most public buildings and attractions are wheelchair accessible.

o Check the City of Vancouver's website (www.vancouver.ca/accessibility) for information.

Disability Alliance BC (📞 604-875-0188; www.disabilityalliancebc.org) Support for people with disabilities.

CNIB (📞 604-431-2121; www.cnib.ca) Support and services for the visually impaired.

Western Institute for the Deaf & Hard of Hearing (📞 604-736-7391; www.widhh.com) Interpreter services and resources for the hearing impaired.

Business Hours

Some attractions, reduce their hours slightly outside the summer.

Banks 9am to 5pm weekdays, some open Saturday mornings.

Shops 10am to 6pm Monday to Saturday; noon to 5pm Sunday.

Restaurants 11:30am to 3pm and 5pm to 10pm.

Coffee shops and cafes From 8am, some earlier.

Pubs and bars Pubs open from 11:30am; bars open from 5pm. Close midnight or later.

Discount Cards

Vancouver City Passport (www.citypassports.com; $29.95) Discounts at attractions, restaurants and activities for up to two adults and two children.

Vanier Park Explore Pass (www.spacecentre.ca/explore-pass; adult/child $42.50/36.40) Combined entry to the Museum of Vancouver (MOV), Vancouver Maritime Museum and HR MacMillan Space Centre is available at any of the three sites. There is also a separate **Dual Pass** (adult/child $31.50/18.50) covering the MOV and Space

Centre.

UBC Museums Pass (adult/child/family $25/20/60) Combined entry to the Museum of Anthropology and Beaty Biodiversity Museum plus 10% discount in their gift shops.

UBC Gardens and MOA Pass (adult/child/family $27/23/65) Combined entry to the Museum of Anthropology (MOA), UBC Botanical Garden and Nitobe Memorial Garden plus 10% discount in their gift shops.

Vancouver Attractions Group (www.vancouverattractions.com) Coupons and discounted entry tickets for multiple attractions.

Electricity

Type A
120V/60Hz

Type B
120V/60Hz

Emergencies

**Police, Fire &
Ambulance** (📞 911)

Money

Credit Cards

o Visa, MasterCard and American Express are widely accepted.

o Credit cards can get you cash advances at bank ATMs, usually for an additional surcharge.

o Many US-based credit cards often convert foreign charges using unfavorable exchange rates.

Changing Money

o You can exchange currency at most main bank branches, which often charge less than the *bureaux de change* dotted around the city.

o In addition to the banks, try **Vancouver Bullion & Currency Exchange** (Map p42; 📞 604-685-1008; www.vbce.ca; 800 W Pender St, Downtown; 🕗 8:30am-5pm Mon-Fri; **S** Granville), which often offers a wider range of currencies and competitive rates.

ATMs

o Interbank ATM exchange rates usually beat the rates offered for traveler's checks or foreign currency.

o Canadian ATM fees are low, but your home bank may charge another fee on top of that.

o Some ATM machines dispense US currency.

Tipping

Restaurants 15% to 18%

Bar servers $1 per drink

Bellhops $2 per bag

Taxis 10% to 15%

Public Holidays

During national public holidays, banks, schools and government offices are closed, and transport, museums and other services often operate on Sunday schedules. Major public holidays in Vancouver:

New Year's Day January 1

Family Day Third Monday in February

Good Friday & Easter Monday Late March to mid-April

Victoria Day Third Monday in May

Canada Day July 1

BC Day First Monday in August

Labour Day First Monday in September

Thanksgiving Second Monday in October

Remembrance Day November 11

Christmas Day December 25

Boxing Day December 26

Responsible Travel

Overtourism

o Visit Vancouver during less busy months such as April/May or September/October and you'll find lower accommodation costs and less crowded attractions.

∘ Plan days out in quieter Vancouver areas such as Kitsilano or the University of British Columbia (UBC) campus.

∘ Slow down and savour the wider Metro Vancouver region. Consider the North Shore for scenic hikes and Richmond for amazing Asian dining.

Lighter Footprints

∘ A car is not required. Neighborhoods including Gastown, Yaletown and the West End are a short walk from downtown and are best explored on foot. The public transit system offers user-friendly services to Kitsilano, Main Street, Granville Island and beyond.

∘ Support businesses that source locally. Shop for gifts at independent artisan stores and buy food and produce at area farmers' markets.

∘ Plastic shopping bags, styrofoam food containers and plastic drinking straws are banned. Businesses charge extra for single-use beverage cups. Plan ahead and bring reusable equipment.

Safe Travel

Vancouver is relatively safe for visitors.

∘ Purse-snatching and pickpocketing do occur; be vigilant with your personal possessions.

∘ Theft from unattended cars is not uncommon; never leave valuables in vehicles where they can be seen.

∘ Street begging is an issue for some visitors; just say 'Sorry' and pass on.

∘ A small group of scam artists works the downtown core, singling out tourists asking for 'help to get back home'. Do not let them engage you in conversation.

∘ BC's COVID-19 regulations continue to evolve. At time of writing, the province's public mask mandate and requirement to show proof of vaccination had both been lifted. International visitors arriving at the Canadian border are still required to prove their full vaccination status. For the latest COVID-19 information, see hellobc.com/know-before-you-go.

Telephone

Most Vancouver phone numbers have the area code ☑604; you can also expect to see ☑778. Dial all 10 digits of a given phone number, including the three-digit area code and seven-digit number.

Cell Phones

Local SIM cards may be used with some international phones. Roaming can be expensive: check with your service provider.

Tourist Information

Tourism Vancouver Visitor Centre (Map p42, G4; ☑ 604-683-2000; www.tourism-vancouver.com; 200 Burrard St, Downtown; ⊙9am-5pm; ⓢ Waterfront) provides free maps, visitor guides, accommodations and tour bookings.

Visas

For more information on visas, see p26.

Behind the Scenes

Send Us Your Feedback

We love to hear from travelers – your comments help make our books better. We read every word, and we guarantee that your feedback goes straight to the authors. Visit **lonelyplanet.com/contact** to submit your updates and suggestions.

Note: We may edit, reproduce and incorporate your comments in Lonely Planet products such as guidebooks, websites and digital products, so let us know if you are happy to have your name acknowledged. For a copy of our privacy policy visit lonelyplanet.com/legal.

John's Thanks

Heartfelt thanks to Maggie for joining me at all those restaurants and for keeping me calm during the brain-throbbing final write-up phase of this project. Thanks to Max, our crazy-whiskered ginger cat, for sticking by my desk . Cheers also to my brother Michael for visiting from England and checking out some local breweries with me: you really know how to go the extra mile.

Acknowledgements

Cover photograph: Vancouver Steam Clock, Jaromir Vanek/ Shutterstock ©.

Back cover photograph: Vancouver Art Gallery, Lissandra Melo/ Shutterstock ©.

Photographs pp28-29 (clockwise from left): Ric Jacyno/Shutterstock ©, Lissandra Melo/Shutterstock ©, peterspiro/Getty ©

This Book

This 4th edition of Lonely Planet's *Pocket Vancouver* guidebook was researched and written by John Lee. The previous edition was also written by John. This guidebook was produced by the following:

Senior Product Editors
Angela Tinson, Martine Power, Saralinda Turner

Cartographers
Rachel Imeson, Corey Hutchison

Product Editors
Sarah Farrell, Alison Ridgway

Book Designers
Norma Prause-Brewer, Fergal Condon

Assisting Editors Michelle Bennett, Ben Buckner, Michelle Coxall, Lucy Cowie, Barbara Delissen, Emma Gibbs, Jodie Martire, Charlotte Orr

Cover Researchers
Gwen Cotter, Meri Blazevski

Thanks to Ronan Abayawickrema, Sonia Kapoor, Kate Mathews, James Smart, Imogen Bannister

Index

See also separate subindexes for:

⊗ **Eating p158**

◯ **Drinking p159**

✪ **Entertainment p159**

🔒 **Shopping p159**

Sights 000
Map Pages **000**

Our Writer

John Lee

Living in Vancouver, John specializes in travel writing and has contributed to more than 150 different publications around the world. These include the *Guardian, Independent, Los Angeles Times, Chicago Tribune, Sydney Morning Herald, National Geographic Traveler* and BBC.com. He also has a travel column in Canada's *Globe and Mail* national newspaper. You can read some of his stories (and see some of his videos) at http://www.johnleewriter.com John has worked on about 25 Lonely Planet books, including *Canada, British Columbia, Western Europe, Vancouver* and *Europe on a Shoestring*.

Published by Lonely Planet Global Limited
CRN 554153
4th edition – Nov 2022
ISBN 978 1 78868 453 8
© Lonely Planet 2022 Photographs © as indicated 2022
10 9 8 7 6 5 4 3 2 1
Printed in Singapore